Vanessa Agnew (ed.)
What We Brought with Us

**The Academy in Exile Book Series** | Volume 3

**Editorial**

The Academy in Exile Book Series is edited by Vanessa Agnew, Kader Konuk, and Egemen Özbek.

**Vanessa Agnew** is a Professor in the Cultural Studies Faculty at Technische Universität Dortmund and is an Honorary Professor in the Humanities Research Centre at the Australian National University. She did a PhD in European studies at the University of Wales, and was tenured in German studies at the University of Michigan. She is Associate Director of Academy in Exile, which supports scholars and cultural producers who have been forced to flee their home countries by authoritarian governments. Her research deals with forced migration, genocide, memory and commemoration, historical reenactment, music history, and ecology.

Vanessa Agnew (ed.)
# What We Brought with Us
Things of Exile and Migration

[transcript]

The publication of this volume has been funded by The Mellon Foundation and Open Society Foundations.

**Bibliographic information published by the Deutsche Nationalbibliothek**
The Deutsche Nationalbibliothek lists this publication in the Deutsche Nationalbibliografie; detailed bibliographic data are available in the Internet at https://dnb.dnb.de/

This work is licensed under the Creative Commons Attribution-NonCommercial-NoDerivatives 4.0 (BY-NC-ND) which means that the text may be used for non-commercial purposes, provided credit is given to the author.
https://creativecommons.org/licenses/by-nc-nd/4.0/
To create an adaptation, translation, or derivative of the original work and for commercial use, further permission is required and can be obtained by contacting rights@transcript-publishing.com
Creative Commons license terms for re-use do not apply to any content (such as graphs, figures, photos, excerpts, etc.) not original to the Open Access publication and further permission may be required from the rights holder. The obligation to research and clear permission lies solely with the party re-using the material.

**First published in 2024 by transcript Verlag, Bielefeld**
© **Vanessa Agnew (ed.)**

Cover layout: Maria Arndt, Bielefeld
Cover illustration: R.B. Kitaj, "Cecil Court, London W.C.2. (The Refugees)," 1983–4, oil paint on canvas, 1830 x 1830 mm. Photograph Courtesy of Tate Images
Copy-editing: Erin Maher
Proofreading: Erin Maher
Printed by: Majuskel Medienproduktion GmbH, Wetzlar
https://doi.org/10.14361/9783839471166
Print-ISBN: 978-3-8376-7116-2
PDF-ISBN: 978-3-8394-7116-6
ISSN of series: 2701-8970
eISSN of series: 2747-318X

*For the little boy who packed a stick and called it a buffalo gun, and his little boy whose journey is just starting.*

*In memoriam Patricia J. Agnew (1937–2024), who took shoes in many sizes.*

# Contents

List of Figures ............................................................. 9

**Lists of Things**
Vanessa Agnew ........................................................... 13

**What Was Left, What Was Saved: Reflections on Jewish Objects of Migration**
Alma-Elisa Kittner ........................................................ 27

**Objects in Transition**
Gisela Ecker ............................................................... 41

**Exile Things**
Academy in Exile Contributors ........................................... 53

**Art Market as Community Builder:**
**Empowering the Makers of Welcome Editions**
Kate Bonansinga .......................................................... 133

**Amy Conger's Double Exile**
Amy Lind .................................................................. 149

**What Matters to Boatpeople: Shirts, Spoons, and Sleep**
*Kim Huynh* ............................................................... 159

**Acknowledgments** ...................................................... 175

**Contributor Biographies** ................................................ 177

**Index** ................................................................... 183

# List of Figures

Figure 1.1: List of Possessions. Helga Weissová, *Zeichne, was Du siehst / Draw what you see: Zeichnungen eines Kindes aus Theresienstadt / Terezín*. Edited by Niedersächsischer Verein zur Förderung von Theresienstadt / Terezín e.V. Source: Photograph courtesy of Wallstein Verlag, Göttingen 1998.

Figure 2.1: Sigmund Freud's writing desk in his office in Vienna as it looked in 1938, before his emigration to England when Germany annexed Austria. Freud's books were labeled "Jewish Science" and burned by Nazis. Photograph courtesy of The Everett Collection.

Figure 2.2: Sophie Calle, *The Wedding Dress*, Appointment with Sigmund Freud, Freud Museum London, 1999. Photograph courtesy of VG Bild-Kunst, Bonn 2023.

Figures in Chapter 4: Photographs by Jobst von Kunowski, courtesy of Academy in Exile.

    Figure 4.1. Child's shoe
    Figure 4.2. A pair of sandals, a souvenir from Grandpa
    Figure 4.3. T-shirt
    Figure 4.4. Dupatta
    Figure 4.5. Traditional tunic
    Figure 4.6. White fabric
    Figure 4.7. Sock
    Figure 4.8. Glasses stand
    Figure 4.9. Watch
    Figure 4.10. Bracelet and watch
    Figure 4.11. Alarm clock

Figure 4.12. Torch
Figure 4.13. Ring
Figure 4.14. Necklace
Figure 4.15. Parting gifts
Figure 4.16. Soft little toy
Figure 4.17. Postcard
Figure 4.18. Fountain pen
Figure 4.19. Letter
Figure 4.20. Books
Figure 4.21. Notebooks
Figure 4.22. Kitschy photo
Figure 4.23. Pictures of an old man with a cat and a hand-embroidered scarf
Figure 4.24. Oil painting
Figure 4.25. Queer flag
Figure 4.26. Keypad phone
Figure 4.27. Afghan flag
Figure 4.28. Venetian silk purse
Figure 4.29. Fur
Figure 4.30. Coffee cups
Figure 4.31. Ultrasound
Figure 4.32. Toy bear
Figure 4.33. Green frog
Figure 4.34. Amber with embedded insects
Figure 4.35. Amulet
Figure 4.36. Keychain
Figure 4.37. Indian misbaha
Figure 4.38. Syrian misbaha
Figure 5.1: Lorena Molina, *At what cost?*, Welcome Edition #8, duotone print, embroidery, walnut frame, 2023, edition of 6, 21"H X 30"W. Embroidery completed by Marelin Cruz, Elia Martinez, Fabiola Rodriguez, Jetzabel Rojas, and Raquel Sotelo. Photograph courtesy of Wave Pool.
Figure 5.2: Lorena Molina, *Do you feel safe?*, Welcome Edition #8, duotone print, embroidery, walnut frame, 2023, edition of 6, 18"H X 30"W.

Embroidery completed by Marelin Cruz, Elia Martinez, Fabiola Rodriguez, Jetzabel Rojas, and Raquel Sotelo. Photograph courtesy of Wave Pool.

Figure 5.3: Lorena Molina, *For who?*, Welcome Edition #8, duotone print, embroidery, walnut frame, 2023, edition of 6, 18"H X 30"W. Embroidery completed by Marelin Cruz, Elia Martinez, Fabiola Rodriguez, Jetzabel Rojas, and Raquel Sotelo. Photograph courtesy of Wave Pool.

Figure 5.4: Lorena Molina, *Do you feel free?*, Welcome Edition #8, duotone print, embroidery, walnut frame, 2023, edition of 6, 18"H X 30"W. Embroidery completed by Marelin Cruz, Elia Martinez, Fabiola Rodriguez, Jetzabel Rojas, and Raquel Sotelo. Photograph courtesy of Wave Pool.

Figure 5.5: Welcome Editions booth at Expo Chicago 2023. Photograph courtesy of Wave Pool.

Figure 5.6: Baseera Khan, *Muslims=America*, Welcome Edition #7, wool, 2022, edition of 13, 36"H X 24"W. A group of five Bhutanese refugee women living in Cincinnati produced this edition with Khan. Weaving work done by Gita Rai, Durga Limbu, Bishnu Limbu, Laxmi Rai, and Sita Gurung with the assistance and training of Rowe Schnure. Embroidery by Fabiola Rodriguez. Photograph courtesy of Wave Pool.

Figure 5.7: Vanessa German, *a holy blue togetherness for planetary awareness of the single universal breath*, Welcome Edition #6 (front), mixed media, 2022, edition of 10, approximately 15"H X 12"W X 10"D. Bead weavings by Bhutanese refugee artists; ceramic works by differently abled artists of Visionaries and Voices; wood carvings by a Nigerian sculptor; hand-dyed prayer beads created by a Zimbabwean artist; glass blowing, cement work, and other pieces created by Cincinnati artists. Photograph courtesy of Wave Pool.

Figure 5.8: Jeffrey Gibson, *Let Me Be Who You Need Me to Be*, Welcome Edition #5, 8/2 Tencel weft with a cotton warp, cherry finished pieces are 17"W x 21"H X 17"W. The weavers were Sita Gurung, Kumari Subba, Bishnu Limbu, Phampa Rai, and Bella Adidjatou. Artist Rowe Schnure helped lead the project along with Susmita Subba and Cal Cullen. Photograph courtesy of Wave Pool.

Figure 6.1. Amy Conger, Untitled. By permission of the estate of Amy Conger.

Figures in Chapter 7: Photographs courtesy of Kim Huynh's family archive.

Figure 7.1. The Huynh family, 1975. Author's family archive.

Figure 7.2. The shirt that Kim Huynh wore when he escaped Vietnam. Author's family archive.

Figure 7.3. The Huynh family's spoon. Author's family archive.

Figure 7.4. UNHCR Displaced Persons Registration Card. Author's family archive.

# Lists of Things

*Vanessa Agnew*

> *Inventory*
> House without roof, child without bed, table without bread, star without light.
> River without bridge, mountain without rope, foot without shoe, flight without destination.
> Roof without house, city without friend, mouth without word, forest without scent.
> Bread without table, bed without child, word without mouth, destination without flight.
> *(Mascha Kaléko 1985, 159; author's translation)*

In 1943, a year after being deported to the Terezín (Theresienstadt) concentration camp, the young Helga Weissová (b. 1929) did a watercolor painting of her parents in their Prague flat.[1] Her father, wearing a suit with a yellow star sewn onto his jacket front, hunches over a writing desk. Her mother, behind him, is bent over a chest of drawers full of linens bundled by pink ribbons, which she is piling on a stool and chair. Although the parents have their backs to one another, there is a tension between them as they engage in separate but shared tasks: he, in his scrawling hand, is making lists of the things that she removes from the drawers. List upon list has accumulated on the desk, suggesting that the

---

1  Following the terminology used by Leo Baeck, Terezín/Theresienstadt, where tens of thousands of people died and whence tens of thousands were sent to be killed, is referred to here as a concentration camp rather than as a ghetto or transit camp.

pair of them have been at it for some time—she sorting, he listing (Fig. 1.1).

*Figure 1.1: Helga Weissová,* List of Possessions.

Source: Courtesy of Wallstein Verlag

Already precocious with brush and pen, Weissová demonstrates a sophisticated perspective—located not, as might be expected of a child, from below or at head height, but from above. The furniture is angled away from the viewer, situating the vanishing point to the right and outside the frame of the painting so that the viewer's eye is drawn into the disoriented scene. We look, with the young painter, down upon the parents from our vantage in the present, as though through a window into the past where we are made privy to a moment of preparedness. The limited color palette of grey, green, and russet tones suggests that it may be evening. Is it late? Are the couple in a hurry? Are they dressed to leave? All we know is that the painting has captured a moment in which Weissová's subjects anticipate one future—a future in which preparedness will provide a safeguard against the unknown—while the viewer anticipates another, more calamitous outcome. This example of visual irony points simultaneously backwards and forwards in time, effectively ruling out the possibility that inventories can play a role in managing events that are yet to occur. Rather than functioning as a form of contingency planning, the making of lists merely captures the instant after which everything will irrevocably change.

Weissová's wartime paintings, of which there are some one hundred, depict the mechanics of life and death in three of the concentration camps where she was incarcerated. In her work, arrivals to Terezín can be seen struggling with their bundles of possessions, queueing for food, scavenging, huddling against the cold, crammed into sleeping quarters, cleaning, picking lice and fleas, and succumbing to diseases like typhoid and tuberculosis. As she shows, the camp prisoners also dream of better times, of plentiful food, family celebrations, and the return home; in Terezín, they can be seen celebrating holidays like Chanukah and organizing concerts and operas (Weissová 1998).[2]

The family spent some three years together in Terezín before Weissová's father was put on a so-called *Osttransport*, a transport to the East. Weissová and her mother would soon follow, being transported first to Auschwitz, and then to concentration camps in Freiberg and Mauthausen (Vaughan 2014). After the war, mother and daughter would return to Prague. Their possessions—inventoried by the parents and the inventorying inventoried by the daughter—had in the meantime been confiscated, stolen, destroyed, lost (Vaughan 2014). Mother and daughter returned to the emptied apartment, where Weissová eventually married and raised her own family, and where she continued to live into advanced old age. The apartment came to be filled with new things, not of the past but redolent thereof. As before, there was a piano; there

---

2 On cultural life in Terezín, see Adler (2017), chapter 19. Specifically, on artwork produced by children in the camp, see Rogoff (2019) and Dutlinger (2001), and on the role played by the artist Friedl Dicker-Brandeis in teaching art to the camp's children, see Wlaschek in Weissová (1998, 148), according to whom Weissová was not taught.

were rugs and paintings and a vase of flowers (photograph, Vaughan 2014). "I am attached to the apartment," she said in a 2014 interview, explaining her decision to remain living there. "Nothing was left, none of our possessions. But the memories were here" (Vaughan 2014).

In relation to her painting "List of Possessions," Weissová explained that preparedness was important. "It's better to be ready and not go anywhere than to get the transport unexpectedly." She went on to describe what this preparedness entailed:

> And so Jewish flats are turning slowly, or actually quite quickly, into warehouses of things needed for the journey. All the Jewish flats have been turned upside down, and ours is no exception. Everywhere—on tables, the chairs and the ground—are stacked suitcases, rucksacks, haversacks, sleeping bags, warm underwear, sturdy shoes, flasks, mess tins, torches, pocket first-aid kits, canteens, solid alcohol, candles... Everyone is getting ready for travel. (Weiss 2014, 21–22)

If her parents were concerned mainly with practicalities, for the child artist, decisions centered on toys. She and her friend agonized over which dolls to choose and how to prevent them being lost or confiscated. Favorite dolls were best hidden in her friend's coat pockets, they decided (Weiss 2014, 26).

The historian of Terezín H. G. Adler shows that regulations stipulated what could be taken on the transports ("only items of practical use," weighing up to 50 kg), while other regulations specified what was to be included in the owner's "hand luggage" (personal documents, passports, ration cards, IDs, bank books, jewelry, and insurance policies) (2017, 57–59). All remaining household possessions had to be listed on an extensive "Property Declaration" form that included "Home Furnishings and Household Items" (Adler 2017, 57–59). It is this that Weissová documents in her painting when she recalls that Jews were forced to submit an inventory of their property to the authorities (1998, 19). Having been forced to turn these inventories over to the authorities prior to leaving ("The property left behind in the homes of the evacuated Jews will be confiscated after their deportation") (G. Weiss, cited in Adler 2017, 795), by mid-1942, all "accompanying luggage" on the transports was being confiscated and plundered as well (Adler 2017, 229, 608). These lists were no trivial thing. Adler concludes that the property declarations were instrumental in dispossessing Jews of their property, while the lists "registering" Jews were preparatory to the deportations (2017, 11), and so, by extension, preparatory to their deaths.

In some sense, then, equivalences were struck between things and people in the totalizing logic of the National Socialist system: people and their possessions were subjected to lists from which narrower selections could be made concerning what was to be retained and who was to survive. The sorting, listing, labeling, and documenting created an illusion of an object's history of rightful ownership—its provenance—as well as of existential continuity. To be listed was potentially to be preserved and to survive. Conversely, when officials in a Nazi extermination camp like Stutthof issued documents stating that no belongings had been transferred ("Keine Effekten übersandt") (Kwiet 2019), it was a cynical pronouncement on the fate of their owners in an extermination camp, where the non-transferal of personal effects signified the likely murder of their owners. For Weissová, the listing of household goods created a rupture: what had been meticulously catalogued by her mother and her father ensured neither continuity of ownership nor guarantee of survival. To the contrary, the list only expedited a certain kind of fate. "No, we never learned what happened to [my father]," Weissová would tell an interviewer in 2014, "because after the war we looked at all the lists, but we never found his name" (Vaughan 2014).

The importance of lists in Weissová's visual and literary accounts of the Holocaust warrants a closer look at what is meant by her term "inventory." By definition, the inventory is a list of a person's property, their "goods and chattels, or parcels of land" (*Oxford English Dictionary* 2023). According to conventional definitions, the inventory includes a determination of each item's purpose, meaning, and worth. Since the early modern period, making inventories has thus been associated with wills and testaments and hence with the transfer of property between heirs or between the individual and the state. More figuratively, the inventory is associated with cataloguing people's things and their properties. Travelers to foreign places, for instance, were enjoined to compile "inventories" of those places by surveying a place's natural resources, its peoples and their practices (*Oxford English Dictionary* 2023). As a kind of proto-apodemic, or set of travel instructions, the inventory was not only a way of cataloguing what was potentially useful and exploitable but also a means of systematizing knowledge making. In formal terms, the inventory attempted to capture the totality of all that was worthwhile and materially valuable. Significantly, according to early definitions, the inventory was made "after [a person's] death or upon their conviction" (*Oxford English Dictionary* 2023). Preserved in the etymology of the word, then, is the sense that the inventory not only has an epistemological status in so far as it helps systematize knowledge making; it also connects to an ontological category that marks a change of state—whether from liberty to incarceration and life to death or, for the purposes of this analysis, from being settled to itinerant and emplaced to displaced.[3]

It is the inventory's relation to shifts in place, time, and being that is useful for our analysis of cultural production associated with flight and migration.[4] In contradistinction to studies of things in themselves, of material culture, and of objects' biographies and their imputed agency in the world (Appadurai 1986; Thomas 1991; Brown 2015), under discussion here is the representation of people's things in novels, memoirs, and art work dealing with forced migration and exile.[5] The things that are described and catalogued in these works stand in for the fullness and roundness of people's lives. These works thematizing the inventory show that to list things is to distill from a much broader set, the subset of what was meaningful and which constituted the owner's peculiar view on the world. The present inquiry into the depiction and function of inventories picks up on an idea in the novelist Abdulrazak Gurnah's *By the Sea*

---

3   On emplacement versus displacement, see Agnew (2020).
4   On the choice of the term "inventory" by artists Massimo Ricciado and Thomas Kilpper for their installation archiving objects taken by refugees across the Mediterranean, see Kittner (2021).
5   On the terminology "things of exile" and "objects in/of exile," see Bischoff and Schlör (2015) and Rossetto and Tartakowsky (2021).

(2001),[6] in which the main character describes himself in "not simple" terms as a "refugee, an asylum seeker" who, like many others, has arrived in a strange place "carrying little bits of jumbled luggage and secret and garbled ambitions" (4). In his encounter with the immigration official inspecting his one precious thing, a box of incense, the character imagines himself subjected to a "hermeneutics of baggage that is like following an archeological trail or examining lines on a shipping map" (7).

Following Gurnah's observation that the border arrival's things are subject to scrutiny and meaning making, this introduction—and, by extension, this volume—asks what a capacious, non-securitized "hermeneutics of baggage" might look like in relation to the forcibly displaced. In dialogue, rather than being at odds with the displaced, interpreting people's things holds a promise of reconstructed refugee routes, as well as possibilities for a deep dive into personal history, as Amy Lind shows of her relative in her chapter on the art historian and photographer Amy Conger's "double exile" from Chile and her home country, the United States. In the proposed hermeneutics of baggage lies a possibility for interpreting that extrapolates from the things people carried or intended to carry. Such a mode of interpreting looks backwards and forwards, examining the life that came before and the death, or possibilities for life, in what came after, all mediated through lists of things. For Alma-Elisa Kittner, writing in this volume about Freud's collection of ethnographic artifacts and classical antiquities, it is the continuity of his inventory taken from Vienna into London exile that allows intellectual work to go on, even while, by implication, the inventory in exile marks a double break from the things' yet-to-be-investigated colonial origins. As Gurnah's "jumbled luggage and secret and garbled ambitions" make clear, however, in any hermeneutics of baggage the possibility of fixing meaning remains elusive: "It was not my life that lay spread there," says the main character of *By the Sea*, "just what I had selected as signals of a story I hoped to convey" (2001, 8).

In what follows, this volume presents a series of case studies, ranging from Nazi Europe (Kittner) to Cold War conflicts in Vietnam (Kim

---

6   I am grateful to Debarati Sanyal for having drawn my attention to this work.

Huynh) and Chile (Lind) as drivers of refugeeism and exile. In the present, global conflict and persecution by authoritarian governments continue to force people from their homes and to frustrate creative and intellectual production ("Exile Things"; Gisela Ecker). As Kate Bonansinga shows, however, artists and makers are using creative work to build community, reshape public perceptions of migrants and refugees, and contribute to a different kind of economic model for artistic production, one based on collaboration. Examining the relation of people's inventories—their baggage—to their intellectual and creative production, the volume tracks their "signals," in Gurnah's words, of untold, or partially told stories. The larger investment in such a project comes from what these inventories tell us not only about individual lives wrenched apart by war and displacement, but also about larger political struggles for democracy, academic and creative freedom, racial justice, economic equality, and gender and sexual diversity and inclusion. As a marker of rupture that demarcates the end of one mode of being and the beginning of another, the inventory, so deeply personal, is also diagnostic. The inventory is conditioned by displacement in space, time, and being. Through its interpretation, we better understand the meaning of that displacement and the possibilities that displacement holds for the future.

*What We Brought with Us*, the project co-curated by the author and Annika Roux, and photographed by Jobst von Kunowski, involved interviewing scholars who had been forced into exile in Germany on account of their intellectual and creative work in repressive countries around the world. Here inventories have been reduced to single, self-selected, and representative things, the significance of which is conveyed in accompanying narratives. Other than by country of origin, contributors are not identified. This is due to the ongoing precarity of their situation, whether as continued potential targets of state-directed harassment or because of their insecure employment and migration status in their host country. Gisela Ecker, writing about this body of work, sets out the various theoretical contexts for interpreting what she refers to as their "objects of transition." Following a material cultural studies approach, these range from "telling objects" (Daston 2004), which have both literal and symbolic meaning, to anthropological ones like Arjun Appadurai's (1998) and David Parkin's (1999), in which things liberated from their original contexts are resettled elsewhere to contribute to a "production of locality."

If creating inventories attempts to regulate the future, inventorying also attempts to manage the past. The pared-down inventory—a shirt and spoon—at the center of Huynh's family story returns us to Gurnah's "signals" of a larger, more complex tale in which possessions have different meanings to different people. Huynh's piece comparing and contrasting the at-odds interpretations of his mother and father serves as an important caution about the overdetermined way in which scholarship sometimes deals with material culture. Objects might stand in for belief systems and human relationships, but they are not the beliefs and relationships themselves. There is value, Huynh implies, in seeing things, literal and figurative, in more than one way.

Freud's list, his reconstructed study in London exile, with its exotic bits and bobs, is predicated on other kinds of lists—the ethnographies and colonial collections that divorced things from their original contexts and removed them to metropolitan centers. For Kittner, of concern is not only the definition of what constitutes a "Jewish" object, but what allows objects of migration to be liberated from their invisibility in the archive or fixity in unchanging collections, and thereby come to "speak." It is through the artist Sophie Calle's engagement with Freud's things, she argues, that Freud's "musealized collection" is finally set in motion.

Lind, in returning to Chile, deals with the most elemental thing of all, human matter, the substance of the person who in exile and as an "inner immigrant" was stripped of the connections to place, social ties, and liberation struggles that were important to her. Conger's inventory has been distilled from a large corpus of photographs, documents, writings, and possessions that had to be abandoned, hidden, and given away when she escaped detainment and torture by the military coup. As against the disappearances practiced by that regime, what Lind returns to Chile to make visible again are vestiges of the self, her aunt's ashes.

## Conclusion

If inventories belong to the dead, imprisoned, and displaced, managing the inventory is the preserve of the living and free. What to take? The question fills the imagination of those who have never been forced to leave their home. Listing and packing are, after all, activities familiar to anyone who has traveled or been inclined to worry about the unforeseen. Making lists hedges against imagined eventualities: the absence of a bed, the need to remain clean, the question of how to navigate new surroundings or find solace in difficult circumstances. With list in hand, packing becomes manageable and, with that, the apparent manageability of an unknown future. Just as the inventory seems to regulate the future, it also invites conjecture. One interview subject, asked about what they would pack were they forced to flee, cast themselves as a *débrouillard*, someone capable of dealing with the exigencies of a life displaced.[7] They would take things useful to survival and conducive to comfort. "Having proper papers with you is also important," they would add, "because getting them replaced is really difficult" (Anonymous 2020), failing to recall that the possession of identifying documents can be a liability in an age of biometric data gathering (known formally in Germany as "Integrated Identity Management") and a securitized asylum process (Federal Office for Migration and Refugees 2024).

What the displaced take with them is thus not necessarily what the emplaced imagine they would take, nor do the things that accompany people correspond to lists made in advance. The lists were too long, things too heavy or impractical; the playing out of possibilities was overtaken by mental anguish and the accelerated time of impending departure. In the end, what was packed was a mish-mash of intention and happenstance. And it is this mish-mash that washes up on the beaches of Dover, Lesbos, Lampedusa, and Possession Island—life jackets, flip-

---

7   Lisa Fittko, the resistance worker who led Walter Benjamin over the Pyrenees in 1940, described the philosopher as lacking a certain adaptability. Schlepping a too-heavy briefcase, he was, she said, "no *débrouillard*" (2022, 154–55). See Taussig's discussion (2006).

flops, fishing tackle, the drowned; it is this mish-mash that can be gathered up in the Sonoran Desert—clothing, ID papers, water bottles, shoes, bones (Undocumented Migrant Project n.d.; De León 2015). For the living, to reconstruct inventories of people's things is to attempt to reconstruct the world as others experienced it. While it is necessary, as Kittner (2021) points out, to preserve the distinction between archives of documented migration and those of undocumented flight, equally important are distinctions between whether things are assumed to have independent agency, speaking for themselves, whether they are spoken about, or, as is largely the case in this volume, whether their meanings are narrated by their owners. As Tiya Miles reminds us, scholarship can draw on multiple types of evidence and archives be read against the grain. Though the lists be short and things few, histories can be compiled even when little remains. From the fabric sack embroidered with its one-time contents and handed from generation to generation, a thick description of an African American family's experience is pieced together in *All That She Carried* (2022) to tell rich stories about slavery and Black women's history.

Even so, perhaps there are also other possessions that were never inventoried and that appear on no lists. In Mascha Kaléko's telling, the inventory is a catalogue of the litotic, describing all that is lost in exile (1985, 159). For those perpetually displaced within Gaza, likely, there are no lists. Compounding the mass loss of life, and creating a condition for genocide, is the destruction of Palestinian cultural heritage in violation of the 1954 Hague Convention for the Protection of Cultural Property in the Event of Armed Conflict (Millender and Lyubasky 2024). What possessions are left to take? For those who do survive, possibly all that remains is intangible heritage, things that are not things, and lists that are not lists of memories, songs, and thoughts.

"We did not weep when we were leaving—for we had neither time nor tears, and there was no farewell." (Muhammed Ali 2006)

## References

Adler, H. G. 2017. *Theresienstadt 1941–1945: The Face of a Coerced Community*. Translated by Belinda Cooper. New York: Cambridge University Press.
Agnew, Vanessa. 2020. "Refugee Routes: Introduction." In *Refugee Routes: Telling, Looking, Protesting, Redressing*, edited by Vanessa Agnew, Kader Konuk, and Jane O. Newman, 13–26. Bielefeld: transcript Verlag.
Anonymous. 2020. Interview conducted by Annika Roux for the *What We Brought with Us* project.
Appadurai, Arjun, ed. 1986. *The Social Life of Things: Commodities in Cultural Perspective*. Cambridge: Cambridge University Press.
Bischoff, Doerte, and Joachim Schlör. 2015. "Dinge des Exils. Zur Einleitung." In *Dinge des Exils*, edited by Doerte Bischoff and Joachim Schlör, 9–20. Munich: Text + Kritik.
Brown, Bill. 2015. *Other Things*. Chicago: University of Chicago Press.
Daston, Lorraine, ed. 2004. *Things That Talk: Object Lessons from Art and Science*. New York: Zone Books.
De León, Jason. 2015. *The Land of Open Graves: Living and Dying on The Migrant Trail*. Oakland: University of California Press.
Dutlinger, Anne D., ed. 2001. *Art, Music and Education as Strategies for Survival: Theresienstadt 1941–45*. New York: Herodias.
Federal Office for Migration and Refugees (BAMF). 2021. "Dossier: Security in the Asylum Procedure." https://www.bamf.de/SharedDocs/Dossiers/EN/Behoerde/sicherheit-im-asylverfahren.html?nn=1279116&cms_pos=1.
Fittko, Lisa. 1985. *Mein Weg über die Pyrenaen: Erinnerungen 1940/41*. Munich: Carl Hanser Verlag.
Gurnah, Abdulrazak. 2001. *By the Sea*. London: Bloomsbury.
Hošková-Weissová, Helga. n.d. "Draw What You See." *Memory of Nations*. https://www.memoryofnations.eu/en/hoskova-weissova-helga-1929.
Kaléko, Mascha. 1985. "Inventar." In *Lyrik des Exils*, edited by Wolfgang Emmerich and Susanne Heil, 159. Stuttgart: Reclam.

Kittner, Alma-Elisa. 2021. "Objects of Migration: On Archives and Collections, Archivists and Collectors." *Visual Anthropology* 34 (4): 385–404.

Kwiet, Konrad. 2019. "Auschwitz: The Exchange of Belongings." Sydney Jewish Museum. https://sydneyjewishmuseum.com.au/news/auschwitz-the-exchange-of-belongings/.

Miles, Tiya. 2022. *All That She Carried: The Journey of Ashley's Sack, a Black Family Keepsake*. New York: Random House.

Millender, Michaela, and Nicolette Lyubarsky. 2024. "When Protectors Become Perpetrators: The Complexity of State Destruction of Cultural Heritage." IPI Global Observatory, April 24, 2024. https://theglobalobservatory.org/2024/04/when-protectors-become-perpetrators-the-complexity-of-state-destruction-of-cultural-heritage/.

Muhammed Ali, Taha. 2006. "There Was No Farewell." In *So What: New and Selected Poems (with a Story), 1971–2005*, translated by Peter Cole, Yahya Hijazi, and Gabriel Levin, 61–62. Port Townsend: Copper Canyon Press.

*Oxford English Dictionary*. 2023. s.v. "inventory." https://www.oed.com/dictionary/inventory_n?tab=meaning_and_use#187699.

Parkin, David. 1999. "Mementoes as Transitional Objects in Human Displacement." *Journal of Material Culture* 4, no. 3 (November): 303–20.

Rogoff, Jana. 2019. "*Butterflies Do Not Live Here* and *On Shoes, Braid and Dummy*: Production and Reception History of Two Czechoslovak Documentaries on the Holocaust." *Apparatus: Film, Media and Digital Cultures in Central and Eastern Europe* 9. http://dx.doi.org/10.17892/app.2019.0009.180.

Rossetto, Piera, and Ewa Tartakowsky. 2021. "The Materialities of Be-longing: Objects in/of Exile across the Mediterranean." *Mobile Culture Studies: The Journal* 7:7–16.

Taussig, Michael. 2006. *Walter Benjamin's Grave*. Chicago: University of Chicago Press. https://press.uchicago.edu/Misc/Chicago/790045.html.

Thomas, Nicholas. 1991. *Entangled Objects: Exchange, Material Culture, and Colonialism in the Pacific*. Cambridge, MA: Harvard University Press.

Undocumented Migrant Project. n.d. https://www.undocumentedmigrationproject.org.

Vaughan, David. 2014. "Helga Weissová-Hošková: Painting the Truth of Terezín." Radio Prague International. https://english.radio.cz/helga-weissova-hoskova-painting-truth-terezin-part-1-8300255.

Weiss, G., ed. n.d. "Einige Dokumente zur Rechtsstellung der Juden und zur Entziehung ihres Vermögens. Schriftenreihe zum Berliner Rückerstattungsrecht. VII." In Adler, *Theresienstadt 1941–1945*, 794–95.

Weiss, Helga. 2013. *Helga's Diary: A Young Girl's Account of Life in a Concentration Camp*. Translated by Neil Bermel. London: Penguin.

Weissová, Helga. 1998. *Zeichne, was du siehst / Draw What You See: Zeichnungen eines Kindes aus Theresienstadt/Terezín*. Edited by Niedersächsischer Verein zur Förderung von Theresienstadt / Terezín e.V. Göttingen: Wallstein.

Wlaschek, Rudolf M. 1998. "Children in the Concentration Camp." In Weissová, *Zeichne, was du siehst / Draw What You See: Zeichnungen eines Kindes aus Theresienstadt/Terezín*, 145–49.

# What Was Left, What Was Saved: Reflections on Jewish Objects of Migration

*Alma-Elisa Kittner*

The interior in which one lives is a playground, limiting and framing one's movements. One arranges oneself and the interior by filling it with objects. It is precisely the rearrangement and reordering of objects, furniture, collected knickknacks, books, clothes—their sorting out, placing, moving again, rearranging or not rearranging—that generates one's own living text, which is rewritten over and over again. It is inescapably linked to the resident who is the author of this text. When one moves, the story usually does not start completely from scratch, but certain aspects of the housing texture remain.

When Sigmund Freud has to emigrate from his home in Vienna to London because the SA is already at his door on 15 March 1938, just one day after the Nazis have marched into Vienna, this is exactly what happens. The flight becomes the occasion for an involuntary repetition: Freud has his Vienna rooms photographically documented and attempts to rebuild his "original study," as James Putnam calls it, in London (Putnam 2005, 154). The new rooms in Hampstead, 20 Maresfield Gardens, become a kind of reenactment of the old ones in Vienna, 19 Berggasse. There, he also places his private collection. The founder of psychoanalysis had placed around three thousand antique and ethnological statuettes, vessels and fragments in his practice rooms in Vienna.[1] These things

---

1   To my knowledge, there has been no research on the colonial context of Freud's collection. The most recent exhibition at the Freud Museum London, *Freud's Antiquity: Object, Idea, Desire*, does not seem to address this either. At the very least,

from the ancient world, primarily Egypt, Mesopotamia, India, and Greece, populated the crowded display cases next to Freud's couch and kept him company on his desk (Fig. 2.1): "My old and dirty gods, so little acknowledged by you," Freud wrote to his friend Wilhelm Fliess in 1899, "take part in the work as manuscript weights" (Freud 1986, 399, translation mine). These are rather inconspicuous artifacts from antiquity, ancient remains, in which Freud's interest in cultural memory structures became apparent and which he even took with him on holiday in part as travel companions (Marinelli 1998b, 11–12). In exchange for paying a so-called *Reichsfluchtsteuer* ("Reich escape tax"),[2] Freud is able to take his ancient Roman, Greek, Egyptian, and Asian figurines and move with them to the new house in London (Davies 1998, 100). Anticipating his approaching death, Freud describes in 1938: "Admittedly, the collection is now dead, nothing more will come to it" (Archive Sigmund Freud Museum Vienna, quoted in Marinelli 1998b, 10, translation mine). In this way Freud points out that a collection must be kept active and alive by constantly changing its objects and therefore its meanings. A year later he dies.

Thus, even before its official musealization, Freud's residence in London is permeated by various stills: by the memory of the old place via photography as a medium of fixation, and by the collection, which per se signifies a form of standing still. It can always be mobilized again, but Freud notices the anticipated end because the collection's order is not set in motion by the acquisition of new pieces. Finally, with Freud's death and later that of his daughter Anna Freud, the transformation of his living space into a museum follows in 1986. The official musealization entails a reordering of the spaces and the things in the spaces. Later on, the curator James Putnam will use these rooms at the Freud Museum in

---

Anna Parker (2023) criticizes in her review of the exhibition that it ignores imperial and colonial networks to which Freud's collection owes its existence. I have a different focus in this essay, but I would like to point out this blank space.

2   In total, Freud's family had to pay a "Reich escape tax" of 31,529 Reichsmark, one-third of the assessed value of their possessions (Davies 1998, 100).

London, with their various layers of stills, to present artistic settings that comment upon and reflect these particular objects collected by Freud.

*Figure 2.1: Sigmund Freud's writing desk in his office in Vienna as it looked in 1938 before his emigration to England when Germany annexed Austria. Freud's books were labeled "Jewish Science" and burned by Nazis.*

Source: Photograph courtesy of The Everett Collection

First of all, it should be noted that with his forced emigration, Freud also takes his objects with him. These are objects that had probably already undergone many migrations,[3] but that migrated again with their owner. On the one hand, these objects include Freud's private collection, which is part of the emigration and is, as such, an object of migration. On the other hand, they also include other objects from his former practice rooms in Vienna. One of the most famous exile objects is also part of Freud's interior: his divan, on which he analyzed his patients. It has

---

3   See note 1.

entered the visual archive of images that appear when psychoanalysis and the so-called "talking cure" come to mind. However, few people are aware that it is an object of migration, located in London and not in Vienna. Time and again, tourists appear at the Sigmund Freud Museum Vienna and miss the famous piece of furniture. Freud's couch appears de-spatialized and de-timed, and the Jewish perspectives on the object are faded out.

## Jewish Objects

Yet can Freud's private collection and his divan be considered Jewish objects of migration? To address this question, it is first necessary to clarify what a "Jewish object" is. Cilly Kugelmann notes critically that not every object that belongs to a Jew automatically becomes a Jewish object (*Jüdische Geschichte Kompakt* 2022). What Gertrud Koch says about films as an object of Jewish studies possibly applies to objects with Jewish connotations: it matters less whether the producers or possessors "belong halakhically,[4] culturally, or ethnically to Judaism; see themselves as Jewish; or are attributed to Judaism by others" (Koch 2021, 429, translation mine). Rather, what is significant is whether the objects "focus on aspects of Jewish life, historical constellations that were decisive for the life of Jewish collectives and individuals" or bring them to the fore in a significant way (ibid.). Therefore, it is essential to make the history of the concrete object transparent and to make clear why this object is in this place at this time and in no other. The fact that Freud's divan and his private collection are in London and not in Vienna is the consequence of his persecution as a Jew and his resulting forced migration. Due to his prominence as an intellectual and the assistance provided by numerous other people, including Marie Bonaparte, he was able to save his life in exile, along with a large portion of his objects. The materiality and the

---

4    Rabbinic Judaism established the halakha, the code of conduct for observant Jews. According to the halakha, a Jew is one who is born by a Jewish mother. Ancient Israel did not know this definition. See von Braun (2021, 15).

history of the objects reveals itself differently in this new living context, even if the auratic power of something like the divan, on which many patients had already lain in Vienna, resonates too.[5] Only by bringing in a Jewish perspective is it possible to perceive the object in all its facets.

In another object from Freud's private collection, by contrast, the Jewishness seems to stand out very clearly: the medieval Hanukkah candelabra, an oil candelabra that hung on the wall (Marinelli 1998a, 153). Like a lot of the objects of his collection, however, it is marked with an inventory number, suggesting that Freud did not understand it as a ritual object but as part of his collection (Marinelli 1998b, 10).

Ceremonial objects like the Hanukkah candelabra that are part of Jewish sacred rituals are usually very decisively perceived as Jewish objects. Yet even here, according to Kugelmann, it is less about the object than about the ceremonial action performed with the object (*Jüdische Geschichte Kompakt* 2022). This is also due to the fact that Jewish culture—with its objects—is deeply routed in experiences of diaspora. The word "diaspora" crystallizes an essential feature of Jewish history: a complex dialectic of exile and domicile (Feierstein 2021, 101). Jewish culture is based on the text as well as the law, which is not territorially anchored. Even a space like the synagogue, according to Feierstein, does not become Jewish through certain characteristics, but through what happens in it, through action: "Doing instead of being, text instead of space" (ibid., 109, translation mine). Accordingly, it is not only the notion of a "Jewish object" that is difficult to grasp, but even the attribution "Jewish." When Jewish culture is regarded as a diasporic one that is less oriented toward space than toward ritual and actions, the question of which objects belong to it can be answered very differently. Various answers are provided by the Jewish museums themselves, which exhibit ceremonial objects as well as objects from the secular Jewish world. Their answers to the question of what is Jewish are also the subject of heated debate (Kugelmann 2021, 500). Thus, what can and cannot be defined as "Jewish" is constantly being renegotiated. This applies equally

---

5    According to Andreas Grote (1994, 14), the "auratic object" refers to a context of meaning and symbolizes a context.

to objects that are not in Jewish museums and yet are located precisely at the interface between the Jewish and non-Jewish worlds—an exchange in which Jewish objects are permanently engaged anyway (Jüdische Geschichte Kompakt 2022). For this reason, when we talk about Jewish objects of migration, we are moving in a field that is not clearly defined.

## Objects of Migration / Objects of Belonging

The dimension of migration with regard to Jewish objects, by the same token, is clearer. As the products of a diasporic culture, Jewish objects have per se been marked by diverse migrations since the destruction of the Second Temple in Jerusalem in the year 70 CE. For the German context and the twentieth century, it is of course relevant that countless objects of Jewish culture were destroyed or dispersed during the Shoah. This is a double loss of things (Jüdische Geschichte Kompakt 2022). Especially after the end of the war in 1945, material evidence of Jewish culture in Germany was almost nonexistent (Kugelmann 2021, 499). This is because, with the Nazi takeover and the persecution and murder of the Jews, as well as the destruction of Jewish culture, the holdings of Jewish museums in Europe were "looted or destroyed, and what remained was distributed to Jewish centers overseas" (ibid., translation mine) This may lead to strange situations in which one has to go to South America, for example, in order to learn about a German-Jewish shoemaker (Jüdische Geschichte Kompakt 2022). Jewish museums in Germany are thus faced with the problem of often having too few or even no artifacts relating to Jewish history and culture. Therefore, it is important to search for objects that still exist but hitherto have not been on display.

Initiatives such as the project "Unboxing Past" by Helgard Haug / Rimini Protokoll, often linked to artistic research, are working on making these visible. In cooperation with the Jewish Museum Frankfurt, the Archaeological Museum Frankfurt, and its archaeologist Thorsten Sonnemann, 513 archive boxes labeled "Synagogue" or "Judengasse" ("Jews' lane") have been opened since mid-2020. They have been in storage at the Archaeological Museum Frankfurt since 1987 and 1990, when the foundations of the synagogue that was destroyed by the Nazis in 1938 and finds from the former "Judengasse" were uncovered during construction work.

After quickly being archived, these objects were not further processed and thus fell into oblivion. The artistic project has now triggered active work on the archive again and accorded it a visual and communicative form. "Unboxing Past" is accompanying the opening of the archive boxes. It initiates public conversations in real or virtual space that deal with questions of personal memory linked to objects. In the course of these conversations, one approaches the objects in the archive box. The work of the archaeologist, who normally works in secret, thus becomes part of a shared social process of remembrance. The forgotten objects of Jewish origin are given a public space again and are remembered.

However, the shards, the tiles, the brutally destroyed Torah shrine, the everyday objects are not so much objects of migration, even if they indirectly point to the forced migration, the flight and deportation of the Jews. Rather, they are objects of belonging. They are things that share a common history with their place of origin: German-Jewish objects from Frankfurt. Violently expelled and destroyed in the past, archived but forgotten for decades, they are now reasserting their place and becoming present. At the same time, they continue to carry their history of destruction with them.

Other objects are also currently becoming present again, especially those from everyday culture that are shaped by Jewish perspectives and histories of migration, even if they cannot be described as "Jewish" per se. Especially in the recent past—such as with the migration of Jews from the former Soviet Union to Germany—a great many everyday objects whose stories are Jewish have migrated with them. Since 2017, the Jewish Museum Berlin has dedicated itself to these objects through the "Object Days" project, under the motto "Show us your story!" So far, more than seventy people have told their stories to the Jewish Museum through objects. "The objects they took with them to Germany—photographs, letters, ceremonial items, dishes, clothing, etc.—illustrate their very personal stories and connections to Judaism" (Gromova, Lewinsky, and Ziehe 2018). Interestingly, it is the declared aim of the

Jewish Museum Berlin to expand its holdings in this way: "The Jewish Museum Berlin intends to acquire more objects related to migration because it has been a constitutive element of the Jewish community in Germany since 1945" (ibid.) The objects are often photographs, items of clothing, pictures, books, and household items such as crockery. They bear witness to former homes, professions, love relationships, friends, and family members. Frequently, they are linked to the history of the Shoah. For example, Viktoria Shtivelman, born in 1940 in Zaporizhzhia (USSR, now Ukraine) and living in Germany since 2002, shows a photo and a wedding cloth:

> The photo shows our family in Omsk during the evacuation in 1944. My parents, my brother, and me. I remember when survivors of the Siege of Leningrad were transferred to Omsk. They couldn't get used to throwing out potato peels. They would wash them and dry them on windowsills. My mother always kept a bag of bread rusks under a bench, which she replaced from time to time, and a bundle of documents. So we could run away with the essentials at any time. The wedding cloth was embroidered by my friend. She gave it to me as a going-away present. This summer, I passed it on to my grandson, to the next generation. A wedding cloth bearing the words "bread" and "salt" is a national [Ukrainian] custom, not a Jewish one. (Ibid.)

The objects take on their meaning through their owner's story. They tell of memory, origin, belonging, of lack and persecution. The "Object Days" project has initiated the significant process of giving voice to the memory of a part of the migrated Jewish community. It is an active attempt to prevent repression and to ensure that important stories are not forgotten and repressed again.

## Artistic Readings of the Objects of Migration

*Figure 2.2: Sophie Calle,* The Wedding Dress, *Appointment with Sigmund Freud, Freud Museum London, 1999.*

Source: © VG Bild-Kunst, Bonn 2023

Sigmund Freud's concern was to use psychoanalysis to create spaces in which something repressed is allowed to come to the fore. He argued that if this does not happen, effective disturbances occur, because the repressed always makes itself felt. Freud's project also had a much larger dimension in mind. He aimed to dissolve not only individual repressions and disturbances, but also social defense mechanisms through the memory work of psychoanalysis. Many artistic positions refer to his concepts of psychoanalytical memory work. Since 1988, the French artist Sophie Calle has been engaging in an artistic form of memory work in her series called "Autobiographical Stories," which she often shows in text-image installations. Her supposedly personal stories become alien stories that are combined with those of other people (Kittner 2009). In an object version of the "Autobiographical Stories," she combines the short, sober texts with mementoes that seem to have personal connotations. With these objects, she also challenges museum displays, such as the Freud Museum in London in the 1999 exhibition "Appointment with Sigmund Freud," curated by James Putnam.

In the form of a wedding dress, her autobiographical story "The Wedding Dress" occupies the most prominent place in the house: the Freudian divan (Fig. 2.2). An old-fashioned white wedding dress can be seen, spread out in full length on the divan. Almost literally, the narrator lies down on Freud's couch as a client. She stages a role-play in a disguise without a body. For this dress, this shell, is the skin of her phantasm, so to speak, as becomes clear in the accompanying story, in which the female protagonist encounters the long-awaited childhood hero in a wedding dress when she becomes his lover:

> I always admired him. Silently, since I was [a] child. One November 8th—I was thirty years old—he allowed me to pay him a visit. He lived several hundred kilometres from Paris. I had brought a wedding dress in my valise, white silk with a short train. I wore it on our first night together. (Calle 2005, 79)

The typological link between childhood and adulthood is specific to Calle's autobiographical narrative perspective. The viewers here are witnesses to a double role-play: the bridal gown of the beloved repeats in adulthood a childhood fantasy, namely the fantasy of appropriating the symbol of femininity that the woman wears at the rite of passage, the wedding and the first night. The symbol of this female metamorphosis now occupies Freud's divan as a client. The autobiographical role-play becomes a cast, the artistic setting a session. The game tips over into an agonal figure: a competition of autobiographically connoted collections emerges and, with it, a competition of authorship. In her appropriation and exaggeration, Calle uses Freud's narrative to establish her own all the more strongly. The frame of his autobiographically coded interior and collection exhibited by the museum, and its authorship, becomes the springboard to install Calle's own authorship. For not only does the artist fit into the Freudian narrative, but the narrative of the psychoanalyst—of which his collection is a part—now always finds its vanishing point in Calle's narratives. On a meta level, however, the typological narrative also thematizes the reciprocal illumination of the present by the past, inspired by Freud. The narrator of Calle's stories acts out her desire to bring the past, which is not past, into the present. The past asserts its place in the installation, literally: the phantasm occupies the divan as a garment cover. In its presence, the object takes the space it needs and is thus metaphorically released to the psychoanalytic pattern of interpretation.

Like many of the artist's object-text installations, the story revolves around the void, the absent: in this case, the absent refers to the artist's body, the body of the lover. This can be interpreted in different ways in the context of visual autobiographies: for example, as the autobiographer's blind spot in her view of herself, as the impossibility of writing, or as showing her own end/death. But through the divan, it is also about the absent Freud and thus indirectly about the Jewishness of the exile object. Calle's story, superimposed on this prominent Jewish exile object, revolves around the very desire whose existence Freud brought to light through psychoanalysis in the first place. It revolves around the mutual illumination of the present by the past and vice versa.

Sophie Calle is not explicitly concerned with the loss of people, places, and objects through the Shoah. Nevertheless, something interesting happened in 2021 when she published the German edition of the "Autobiographical Stories," an artist's book entitled *Wahre Geschichten* ("True Stories"). The book appears to be dedicated to four people: "For Nichouma Krajka and Hélène Sindler, for Szoel Szyndler and Charles Sindler" (Calle 2021). Yet the artist explains in an interview:

> Nichouma Krajka was the name of my Polish-Jewish grandmother, Szoel Szyndler that of my French grandfather. During the war, they changed their names to Hélène and Charles Sindler in order to hide.

I wanted to dedicate this book, this first German edition,[6] to their two identities: the one before the war and the one after. They never got rid of the fear. When I took the Trans-Siberian railway, they asked me not to set foot in either Poland or Germany. I complied and did nothing in Germany for a very long time. Not because of me, I have no problem with that at all, but because of them. For me, dedicating this book to them now is a way of telling them: you don't have to be afraid anymore, it's over, a lot of time has passed, we're going there together now. (Hirsch 2021, translation mine)

Calle herself, the master of playing between facts and fictions who always keeps the audience guessing, openly lays a trail to her Jewish origins here. From this Jewish perspective, her stagings of various voids and absences, her play with identities and maskings could be reinterpreted: behind this lies a specifically Jewish historical experience that corresponds with Freud's experience of persecution and flight. Thus, Freud's object and Calle's object begin to talk to each other. They talk about sexual desire and about the childlike joy of disguises, and at the same time about the absence of loved ones and the need to mask. Calle's "Wedding Dress" makes the divan visible in a new way and sets Freud's musealized collection in motion again. Her artistic intervention shows that objects of migration can be made to speak. However, the reference to their specifically Jewish context leads to other conversations. They unfold the complexity of the objects and show how they connect history and the present.

---

6   This was not the first German edition of the "Autobiographical Stories." In 2004, Calle published *Wahre Geschichten* at the Prestel publishing house. At the time, however, there were only thirty-six stories, while the edition published by Suhrkamp in 2021 contains sixty-five ("Autobiographical Stories" is an ongoing project). The dedication to Calle's grandparents is not present in the earlier edition. It was not until 2021 that Calle felt it was important to make her Jewish origins visible.

## References

Braun, Christina von. 2021. "Die Zugehörigkeit zur jüdischen Gemeinschaft." In *Handbuch Jüdische Studien*, 2nd ed., edited by Christina von Braun and Micha Brumlik, 15–58. Vienna: Böhlau.
Calle, Sophie. 2005. *Appointment with Sigmund Freud*. London: Thames and Hudson/Violette Editions.
Calle, Sophie. 2021. *Wahre Geschichten*. Berlin: Suhrkamp.
Davies, Erica. 1998. "'Eine Welt wie im Traum': Freuds Antikensammlung." In *"Meine … alten und dreckigen Götter": Aus Sigmund Freuds Sammlung*, edited by Lydia Marinelli, 94–101. Frankfurt: Stroemfeld.
Feierstein, Liliana Ruth. 2021. "Diaspora." In *Handbuch Jüdische Studien*, 2nd ed., edited by Christina von Braun and Micha Brumlik, 101–11. Vienna: Böhlau.
Freud, Sigmund. 1986. *Sigmund Freud, Briefe an Wilhelm Fließ 1887–1904*. Edited by Jeffrey Moussaieff Masson. Frankfurt: S. Fischer.
Grote, Andreas. 1994. "Vorrede – Das Objekt als Symbol." In *Macrocosmos in Microcosmo, Die Welt der Stube: Zur Geschichte des Sammelns 1450 bis 1800*, edited by Andreas Grote, 11–20. Opladen: Leske + Budrich.
Kittner, Alma-Elisa. 2009. *Visuelle Autobiographien: Sammeln als Selbstentwurf bei Hannah Höch, Annette Messager und Sophie Calle*. Bielefeld: transcript.
Koch, Gertrud. 2021. "Jüdisches Leben im Film." In *Handbuch Jüdische Studien*, 2nd ed., edited by Christina von Braun and Micha Brumlik, 463–66. Vienna: Böhlau.
Kugelmann, Cilly. 2021. "Jüdische Museen." In *Handbuch Jüdische Studien*, 2nd ed., edited by Christina von Braun and Micha Brumlik, 491–501. Vienna: Böhlau.
Marinelli, Lydia, ed. 1998a. *"Meine … alten und dreckigen Götter": Aus Sigmund Freuds Sammlung*. Frankfurt: Stroemfeld.
Marinelli, Lydia. 1998b. "'Meine … alten und dreckigen Götter': Aus Sigmund Freuds Sammlung." In *"Meine … alten und dreckigen Götter": Aus Sigmund Freuds Sammlung*, edited by Lydia Marinelli, 8–19. Frankfurt: Stroemfeld.

Putnam, James. 2005. Afterword to *Appointment with Sigmund Freud*, by Sophie Calle, 153–54. London: Thames and Hudson/Violette Editions.

## Online References

Gromova, Alina, Tamar Lewinsky, and Theresia Ziehe. 2018. *Object Days. Memorabilia and Migration Stories – Portraits of Jews Living in Germany.* www.jmberlin.de/en/node/5528; https://www.jmberlin.de/en/object-days-bag-of-bread-rusks.

Haug, Helgard. n.d. "Unboxing Past." www.rimini-protokoll.de/website/en/project/unboxing-past.

Hirsch, Annabelle. 2021. "Interview mit Sophie Calle. Die Meisterin der Indiskretion." *Frankfurter Allgemeine Zeitung*, 18 July. https://www.faz.net/aktuell/feuilleton/buecher/interview-mit-der-kuenstlerin-sophie-calle-ueber-wahre-geschichten-17427790.html.

*Jüdische Geschichte Kompakt.* 2022. Episode 25, "Jüdische Objektgeschichte," with Elisabeth Gallas, Cilly Kugelmann, and Miriam Rürup, 6 May. https://juedischegeschichtekompakt.podigee.io/26-podcast-cilly-kugelmann-elisabeth-gallas-miriam-ruerup.

Parker, Anna. 2023. "Freud's Collection Compulsion: The Archaeological Site of Mind." Parapraxis. https://www.parapraxismagazine.com/articles/freuds-collection-compulsion.

# Objects in Transition

*Gisela Ecker*

What we are given to see in *What We Brought with Us* are things[1] chosen by their owners in a state of duress, things chosen to accompany them at a time of dramatic disruption and life-changing upheaval. Separated from their habitual surroundings, these things seemingly have to fulfill a range of purposes that extend from the functional to the emotional and, like their owners, are traveling from one place to another. They are objects in transition. Moreover, they are being presented through photographic representation and in a manner that is, in principle, accessible to everyone. The objects are encompassed by a profoundly generalizable narrative—the exilic condition of their owners—and, in addition, they are accompanied by some basic information about their past and reflections that illuminate why they have been selected and retained.

First shown online as part of the *Re:Writing the Future Festival*, then at the National Literaturarchiv Marbach in Germany, and, in 2023, at the University of Cincinnati's Meyers Gallery and the Goethe-Institut in New York, the *What We Brought with Us* exhibition has had access to a wide public. Most of these viewers have not undergone the dramatic and often traumatizing experience of exile. No doubt their first and most intense reaction derives from a sense of personal identification and compassion

---

1   In this text, I refer to "objects" to aim at generalized aspects and to "things" to highlight connections between thing and person, sometimes even synonymously. The scholarly debate over these terms has not arrived at any single conclusion, and it is beyond the scope of this essay to rehearse the discussion here. For a brief overview, see Candlin and Guins (2009), Part II.

for the exiled owners of these things, prompting the question, "Which things would I choose were I thrown into a situation like this?"

In the exhibition, each object stands out monolithically against a dark background; the photographs are taken with great care and artistic skill, with special attention given to a sense of materiality and the surface qualities of the object. In some cases, such as in the **baby shoe** or **coffee cups**, the mode of ambitious portrayal seems to contradict the worn-out or "ordinary" nature of the thing. The unusual valorization implied in this photographic approach confers and mirrors the revaluation the things have already received by being singled out from their original contexts and chosen as significant objects and companions. In the exhibition catalogue, photographic thumbnails are added to the wide-angle shots of the objects, thereby heightening the impact of each precious thing.

The displayed objects do not share any basic classifications, such as object of use, souvenir, or artifact. Their only common feature is the fate they share with their owners after having been singled out, most probably under great emotional strain, intensified by limitations of time, luggage allowance, and other circumstances.

## "Telling Objects"

Some of the assembled things lend themselves quite easily to a symbolic reading because their type can be found within general (Western) cultural archives and because they have a rich life in poetry and the visual arts. The **torch**, **watch**, and **alarm clock**, for example, are generally seen as wayfinding instruments that allow people to orient themselves in time and space, and thus, as concepts, they inspire further abstraction.[2] Traditional hermeneutics, in fact, tends to assign a more or less fixed meaning to objects in general. This process of attributing meaning to things has been increasingly criticized in recent decades and is even regarded as a potential act of appropriation when applied to material things and

---

2   See, for example, Şenocak (2006).

their living context. Historian of science Lorraine Daston, for example, in her introduction to *Things That Talk* (2004), raises the question of how apparently "speechless" non-human objects can be turned into "telling objects" if asked appropriate questions.[3] As Daston puts it, it is necessary to "confront the paradox head-on and... take it for granted that things are simultaneously material and meaningful" (17). Following Daston's suggestion, one of the demands of such a practice would be ongoing and thorough recontextualization. Simply put, the torch, watch, and alarm clock need not stay fixed in a single category. Symbolic meaning cannot claim to be exhaustive but can easily coexist with other and ever-changing meanings: things can at once be objects of practical use and, simultaneously, serve as reminders of their personally attributed symbolic value.

If we take seriously Daston's claims about things, that "their utterances are never disembodied" and that they "communicate by what they are as well as by how they mean" (20), then material cultural studies has a lot to contribute and many new issues to pursue. This potential can be seen in many of the exhibited things, perhaps most strikingly in the **baby shoe**.

## Mementoes and the "Production of Locality"

To learn more about objects taken along into exile, we have to look at approaches adopted by anthropologists who study transnational movements. With his focus on global population shifts and the subsequent "deterritorialization" of ever-increasing numbers of people, Arjun Appadurai (1998, 27) has opened avenues for looking at both human subjects *and* things in transition. Both "deterritorialization" and subsequent "reterritorialization" are processes that are dramatically shaping our globalized world, with exile being a violent, disrupting, and traumatic manifestation of enforced dislocation and relocation. "Production of locality," the term Appadurai uses to refer to acts of

---

3   See also Kimmich (2011).

reterritorialization (1998, 178–200), distinctly moves us away from the traditional notion of *Heimat* (see Ecker 2012), with its static beliefs about time and homogeneous social structures. Whereas Appadurai's concept of "locality" is viewed "as primarily relational and contextual," the corollary term "neighborhood" refers "to the actually existing social forms in which locality, as a dimension or value, is variably realized" (1998, 178–79). Things play an indispensable role in these processes; people and things are torn away from their habitual surroundings and subsequently become involved in the "production of locality" (178–79), i.e., in actively establishing new neighborhoods in which they will have to find and construct new places where the old and new will mingle and interact with each other.

Whereas migration usually allows for more planning time and larger volumes of things to be transferred across borders, exile is dominated by pressures and extreme restrictions at all levels. The use value of objects (the literature on migration often stereotypically mentions pots and featherbeds) gives way to other forms of value. In his essay on transitional objects, anthropologist David Parkin writes about objects in the context of "forcible human displacement": "items taken under pressure and in crisis set up contexts less of use and more of selective remembering, forgetting and envisioning" (1999, 304). Items come to serve "as mementoes of sentiment and cultural knowledge and yet also as bases of future re-settlement"; in this way, "the 'transitional objects' carried by peoples in crisis inscribe their personhood in flight but offer the possibility of their own de-objectification and re-personalization afterwards" (303). In the eyes of their owners, these mementoes are "inscribed with narrative and sentiment, which may later re-articulate the shifting boundaries of a socio-cultural identity" (313).

Appadurai's and Parkin's positions encompass the past and the projected future of objects in transition along a spatial and temporal axis on both sides of the violent disruption of exile. Torn from their normal existence in ensembles, things will be included in new ensembles where they interrelate with other things in the processes of homemaking. These insights raise many questions to pose to the things isolated by circumstances and gathered in *What We Brought with Us*. From which neighborhood has each object been separated and singled out? We know that they have been highly valorized and selected by their owners, yet which roles did they play in the company of other things and in the context of their original homes? What practical uses, atmospheric and aesthetic value, and familiar patterns and habits in everyday life were accorded them? And subsequently, what will they contribute to the neighborhoods they are about to enter? As objects of transition, they have been excised, artistically portrayed, and exhibited at precisely the moment between these two processes in the "production of locality."

## Biographies of Things

While it may seem like an act of anthropomorphizing, applying notions of a "biography of things" seems particularly appropriate in this context. Igor Kopytoff sketches the issues at stake:

> In doing the biography of a thing, one would ask questions similar to those one asks about people: What, sociologically, are the biographical possibilities inherent in its "status" and in the period and culture, and how are these possibilities realized? Where does the thing come from and who made it? What has been its career so far, and what do people consider to be an ideal career for such things? What are the recognized "ages" or periods in the thing's "life," and what are the cultural markers for them? How does the thing's use change with its age, and what happens to it when it reaches the end of its usefulness? (1986, 66–67)

Within their lifetimes, things rarely remain fixed within a single category but are subject to many shifts in classification (see Hahn 2005, 40–45). Categories, such as household tool, garbage, museum artifact, souvenir, commodity, memento, or gift, do not originate in the things themselves. Rather, they are the result of human attribution, either by explicit labels or implicitly. Such attributions are made according to the ways in which things are used by humans, in keeping with their habits, via the neighborhoods in which they have been positioned, and commensurate with their evaluation by cultural norms that are subject to historical change. The value attached to things is neither totally subjective nor quite objective, for value follows what is generally attributed to things in a specific culture and, in addition, the individual subject creates a personal order within the ensemble of things he or she owns. This fundamental ambivalence becomes heightened if we look at single things taken across borders and into exile.

In her novel *The Museum of Unconditional Surrender*, Dubravka Ugrešić (1996) traces the steps of exiled things and regularly arrives at a world of absences: "Exile is the history of the things we leave behind, of buying and abandoning hair-driers, cheap little radios, coffee pots" (113). Things taken into exile bear witness to loss (see Kimmich 2011, 9–13). Yet to substitute or stand in for what has been left behind is a role too demanding for the things taken on the journey, impossible to fulfill. Maybe this accounts for the aura some of the things seem to radiate.

In general, the lives of things—with their life cycles and paths depending on materiality, on the emotional and practical services they provide—only rarely fully coincide with the biographies of their owners. In contrast, the things under discussion here are destined to share their trajectories most closely with their owners, who have chosen them as portable companions into exile. Thus, at least for the time being, i.e., during the period of passage, most of them have undergone a radical revaluation, even if this act of selection may have been performed under great pressure and more spontaneously and unconsciously than through deliberate calculation. Moreover, it is often only in retrospect that such things can be seen in a different light and move from useful tool to memento. Such a striking change of category is observable in the case of the **white fabric**, originally handed over by the person's mother to secure the suitcase with its broken zip. For me, this is a moving instance of a powerful transformation from useful tool to memento.

## "Transitional Objects" in Psychology

"Transitional objects" is a term originally coined by Donald Winnicott to explain young children's use of objects like blankets and teddy bears to bridge the absence of a caring person. The term has also been found useful in the discussion of forceful separation such as exile, when objects are chosen to provide emotional or practical assistance—to convey a spark of hope and a sense of continuity in situations of despair, upheaval, and disruption from everything that once provided those feelings of security and well-being. In his book *Geliebte Objekte*, psychologist Tilmann Habermas (1999) examines things in people's "emotional households" and provides detailed insights into the uses of objects in situations of extreme change and disruption. Although there are many designations available—for example, "*rite-de-passage* souvenirs"—he, like Parkin (1999), seizes upon "transitional objects" as the appropriate term. According to Habermas's research, things that facilitate transition serve most frequently to carry forward deep-rooted relationships with people who had to be left behind. This is clearly mirrored in *What We Brought with Us*, where it is not merely the thing that is transmitted but the specific relationship that it evokes and the memories contained therein. Specifically, the **torch, watch, alarm clock, handwritten letter, white fabric, dupatta, child's shoe, sock, coffee cups, ultrasound**, and **notebooks** are all accompanied by narratives that highlight special personal relationships. If we look more closely, the majority of these things were given as gifts and thus, according to central notions of gifts and gift-giving, retain something of the giver of the gift, and of his or her intention and personal attitude. Quite similar to processes of mourning, the gift, which once literally rested in the hands of the giver, is believed to retain some of these tactile traces.

Like a powerful framing narrative, the **ultrasound** is especially strong in setting up a sense of continuity between past and present. In the case of the **child's shoe** and the **sock**, there is no possible return to their erstwhile use value, whereby the objects might be carried into everyday life. Within the collection, the pieces of **fur**, specifically, stand out as a form of relic.

"Continuity with oneself" (1999, 302) is the wider concept Habermas considers as the main underlying purpose of transitional objects. This can be found in the ritual function of the **amber**, a function created through habit, and the **T-shirt, dupatta,** and **toy bear**. The carefully wrapped **keypad phone** is destined to serve as a reminder of extreme political repression, whereas the **Venetian silk purse,** like an anecdote, stands for the fraught moment of crossing borders.

## Beyond Nostalgia

As we learn from the accompanying narratives in *What We Brought with Us*, a significant number of things have been chosen because of their value as mementoes. If we look more closely, "memento" can mean many things. The future role of mementoes is frequently seen in their value as nostalgic objects that evoke the past. In her study *The Future of Nostalgia* (2001), Svetlana Boym insists that the popular notion of nostalgia, which tends to idealize the past, has to be expanded beyond its common definition as "a longing for a home that no longer exists or has never existed" (viii). Applied to things taken into exile, such a narrow view of nostalgia is, according to Boym, extremely limiting, for it privileges the idea of a homogeneous cultural sphere in both the past and the present. Such homogenization no longer corresponds to the vast human displacement that characterizes the world today. Finally, things defined as nostalgic objects may end up displayed in what Boym calls "little bookshelf museums" (333). In Boym's research and fieldwork, the stories told by the owners of classical "nostalgic objects" "reveal more about making a home abroad than about reconstructing the original loss" (328): "Diasporic souvenirs do not reconstruct the narrative of one's roots but rather tell the story of exile" (336). She reminds us that mementoes are never just nostalgic objects but are supposed to play a sustaining role in the future life of their owners. The **toy bear**, for example, would certainly deserve a future place on the shelf and serve as a powerful reminder of different phases of the owner's past life. Thus, in looking at *What We Brought with Us*, we may well ask which roles these mementoes will play in the future lives of their owners. Will such things as the **alarm clock** or **keychain** resume their practical uses, on top of remaining a thing that carries loving memories? And will the **sock** be reunited with its counterpart? In contemporary literature,[4] we find countless examples of such a blending and accumulation of services, practical and emotional, in things taken into exile.

## *The Comfort of Things* (Miller 2008)

In Daniel Miller's anthropological study of the things found in households of a randomly selected, "entirely ordinary-looking street" in London, his questions were posed not only to the chosen householders, but also, and mainly, to the things accumulated and positioned in the interiors of the houses—the collections on the mantelpiece or decorations on the wall. His central assumption was that "these things are not a random collection. They have been gradually accumulated as an expression of that person or household. Surely if we can learn to listen to these things we have access to an authentic other voice" (2008, 2). Since most of the residents in his study were marked by personal histories of migration and exile, Miller's fieldwork offers valuable insights into the possible future lives of things once they have been integrated into new ensembles: how things relating to a painful past mingle with others, how they combine emotional reminiscence with practical use, and how they speak of relationships both with people and with each other. Their implicit messages can, in other words, differ from the explicit statements and evaluations made by their owners. Here, we are back to Daston's (2004) seminal position—and also more informative, as, according to Miller, "apparently mute forms can be made to speak more easily and eloquently to the nature of relationships than can those with persons" (287). To their owners, it is exactly the interplay and combination of things—even in, and maybe because of, their repetitive presence—that

---

4   See, for example, the cutting knife in Jhumpa Lahiri's "Mrs. Sen's" (1999) or the handkerchief in Herta Müller's Nobel Prize speech (2009).

provide comfort and a sense of private and safe surroundings. Having learned from Latour (2009) about the complexities of the interplay between humans and non-humans, we find intricate interrelations in the specific context of *What We Brought with Us*: as transitional objects, non-human things have been delegated the immense task of bridging a gaping emotional gap. They have other tasks, too, tasks originating from their biographies. They will continue to shape everyday human actions together with their new non-human companions and speak of embedded lives in narratives enlarging those that derive from their owners.

Again, looking at our collection of "forlorn" and isolated things, the onlookers who have not undergone this experience of dramatic dislocation gain a sense of the enormous losses borne by the subjects of exile. At the same time, these things offer insights into the equally enormous task of re-establishing personal surroundings that provide comfort. Which place and role will our things find in their new neighborhoods of things?

## References

Appadurai, Arjun. 1998. *Modernity at Large: Cultural Dimensions of Globalization*. Minneapolis: University of Minnesota Press.
Bischoff, Doerte, and Joachim Schlör, eds. 2013. *Dinge des Exils*. Exilforschung: Ein internationales Jahrbuch 31. Munich: edition text+kritik.
Boym, Svetlana. 2001. *The Future of Nostalgia*. New York: Basic Books.
Candlin, Fiona, and Raiford Guins, eds. 2009. *The Object Reader*. New York: Routledge.
Daston, Lorraine, ed. 2004. *Things That Talk: Object Lessons from Art and Science*. New York: Zone Books.
Ecker, Gisela. 2012. "Prozesse der 'Beheimatung': Alltags- und Memorialobjekte." In *Heimat: At the Intersection of Memory and Space*, edited by Friederike Eigler and Jens Kugele, 208–25. Berlin: de Gruyter.
Habermas, Tilmann. 1999. *Geliebte Objekte: Symbole und Instrumente der Identitätsbildung*, Frankfurt am Main: Suhrkamp.

Hahn, Hans Peter. 2005. *Materielle Kultur: Eine Einführung*. Berlin: Dietrich Reimer Verlag.

Kimmich, Dorothee. 2011. *Lebendige Dinge in der Moderne*. Konstanz: Konstanz University Press.

Kopytoff, Igor. 1986. "The Cultural Biography of Things: Commoditization as Process." In *The Social Life of Things: Commodities in Cultural Perspective*, edited by Arjun Appadurai, 64–91. Cambridge, Cambridge University Press.

Lahiri, Jhumpa. 1999. "Mrs. Sen's." In *Interpreter of Maladies*, 111–35. Boston: Houghton Mifflin Harcourt.

Latour, Bruno. 2009. "Where Are the Missing Masses? The Sociology of a Few Mundane Artifacts." In *The Object Reader*, edited by Fiona Candlin and Raiford Guins, 229–54. New York: Routledge.

Miller, Daniel. 2008. *The Comfort of Things*. Cambridge: Polity Press.

Müller, Herta. 2009. "Every Word Knows Something of a Vicious Circle." Nobel Lecture, 7 December. https://www.nobelprize.org/uploads/2018/06/muller-lecture_en.pdf.

Parkin, David. 1999. "Mementoes as Transitional Objects in Human Displacement." *Journal of Material Culture* 4, no. 3 (November): 303–20.

Şenocak, Zafer. 2006. "Der Kompass." In *Das Land hinter den Buchstaben: Deutschland und der Islam im Umbruch*, 19–20. Munich: Babel Verlag.

Ugrešić, Dubravka. 1996. *The Museum of Unconditional Surrender*. Translated by Celia Hawkesworth. New York: New Directions.

# Exile Things

*Academy in Exile Contributors*

When people are forced from their homes, their things carry symbolic weight and come to represent the tangle of human relations that constitute an emplaced life. Yet these things also stand for hope: they are a seed that must grow and bear fruit in strange ground. Such things are not necessarily judiciously chosen; they tend to be selected in haste and confusion. *En route*, things may be lost, gifted, and stolen, or jettisoned because they can't be carried any farther. What is retained acquires new meaning and may become the metonym for an entire existence.

Such things can make us question our connection to material possessions and to one another. We are prompted to reflect on what is most precious to us. What single thing stands in for a lost world? Is belonging defined in material terms? What if, in leaving, we can take nothing?

Vanessa Agnew

A selection from "Exile Things" forms the exhibition *What We Brought with Us*. The exhibition presents images of some of the things taken by scholars who left their countries of origin for Germany, where they were hosted by Academy in Exile at the Universität Duisburg-Essen, along with Freie Universität Berlin, Forum Transregionale Studien, and Kulturwissenschaftliches Institut Essen. Academy in Exile is now based at Technische Universität Dortmund, where it continues to support scholars at risk.

*What We Brought with Us* was first shown in the digital *Re:Writing the Future Festival*, subsequently at the Deutsches Literaturarchiv Marbach, The University of Cincinnati, the Goethe-Institut New York, Literaturhaus Berlin, Vilnius Old Town Hall, and elsewhere. The exhibition has been supported by the Universität Duisburg-Essen, Technische Universität Dortmund, Mellon Foundation, VolkswagenStiftung, Open Society Foundations, Allianz Foundation, University Alliance Ruhr, University of Cincinnati, Consortium of Humanities Centers and Institutes, and Goethe-Institut New York, among other institutions. It is shared with concern for those who are forced to live in exile as a result of oppression by authoritarian regimes around the world.

Photographs by Jobst von Kunowski; curated by Vanessa Agnew and Annika Roux

## Child's shoe

This shoe belonged to me when I was a little girl. I found it among my mother's belongings when she died. When I went into exile, it was one of the few things I took as a memento of her. The other shoe is lost.

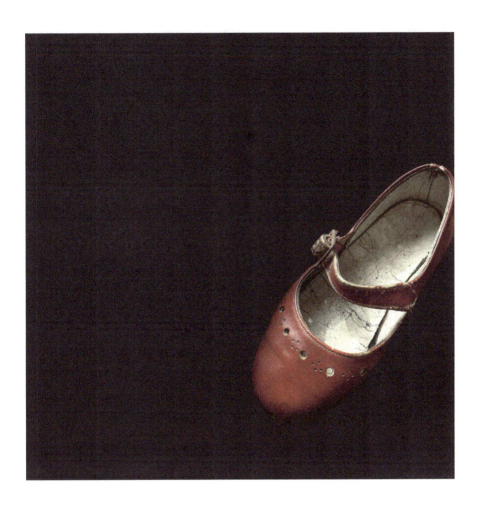

## A pair of sandals, a souvenir from Grandpa

I couldn't be with my grandpa in his final days. This is the last thing he sent me. In looking at the sandals, I recall his words from my childhood, "Always choose the right path and stick to it." Rest in peace, Grandpa.

## T-shirt

This motto was adopted by the pro-democracy movement in Hong Kong. In carrying this T-shirt with me, I hope to spread the spirit of liberty afar. It should serve as a reminder to people who've never lived under an authoritarian regime or had to fight for democratic values. Don't take your freedoms for granted.

Academy in Exile Contributors: Exile Things 61

## Dupatta

I consciously packed this dupatta. My grandmother, my mother, and my aunts all wore wide dupattas. The dupattas were scented differently, though. All of them might wear the same pattern and color, yet one could detect the difference. My grandmother's always has a peculiar mustardy smell, my aunt's a bit nutty, and my mother's smells of something that I have not been able to decipher. Perhaps it's the smell of love. I carried this wide dupatta to remind myself of the smell of love that awaits me somewhere.

Academy in Exile Contributors: Exile Things   63

## Traditional tunic

This is the traditional clothing worn by Afghan men. Such garments are hand-sewn by women and sometimes made of silk. They can be really expensive and are treasured because of all the work that goes into making them. I was given the *kalmeez* by a friend of mine, and before that, it belonged to a bridegroom. Passing on a gift like this is thought to bring luck. I only wear it on special occasions. Hopefully, one day, I too will meet the love of my life and get married.

## White fabric

Before I left, my mother wanted to be sure that my luggage with a broken zip wouldn't burst open, so she tied a white cotton cloth around it.

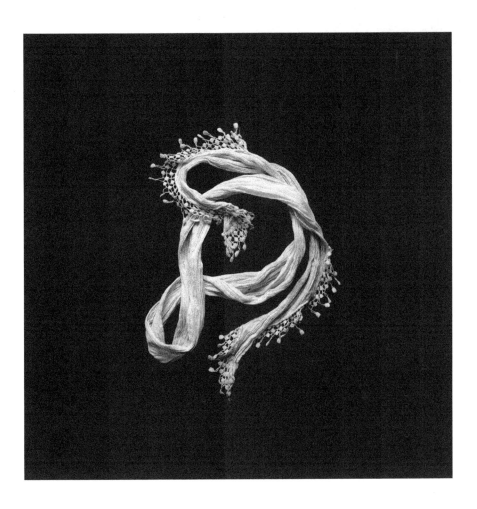

## Sock

Some time ago, a dear friend from London sent me a nice pair of socks as a gift. One day, when I was packing up for a trip to Geneva, I could find only one of the socks. No matter how much I searched, the other one did not appear. Later, it transpired that the missing sock was in my hometown, Istanbul, apparently forgotten there during a visit. Today, one of the socks is in Essen and the other in Istanbul. I feel that I'm not so unlike these socks myself.

—Fırat Erdoğmuş

## Glasses stand

I bought this nose-shaped glasses stand in April 2015 during our visit to Yerevan for the centenary of the Armenian Genocide. The nose belongs to Yeghishe Charents, one of the greatest poets and political activists of Armenia. Born in Kars, Charents sought a *yergir* (homeland) in his works as a way of healing the traumatic loss of home. Here, this object—which, back in our house in Turkey, used to be a souvenir from Armenia—gained significance for us as a symbol of hope that we could make a new home in exile.

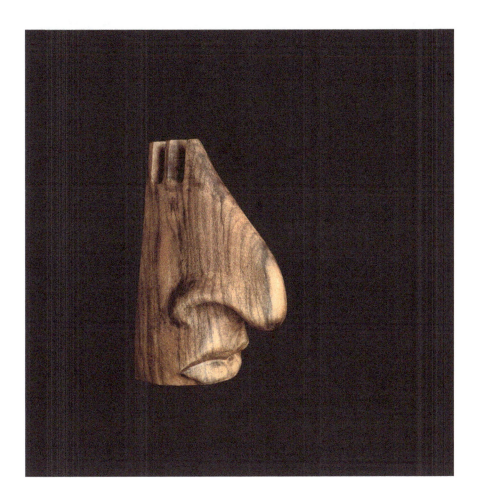

## Watch

My father doesn't give gifts. It's not that he's not generous—he used to give me a quarter of his salary so I could study. But, as a rule, he doesn't make a thing of giving gifts. The watch was his. It's the only actual gift he's given me. It's a reminder of how precious time is.

Academy in Exile Contributors: Exile Things    73

## Bracelet and watch

These things represent the hope my wife and I hold for our reunion. They are the last and loveliest gifts we purchased for one another before I had to flee. We exchanged the gifts: my watch remained in the hands of my wife and her bracelet accompanied me on my enforced journey. No matter what, they will always remind us of love, hope, and the passage of time.

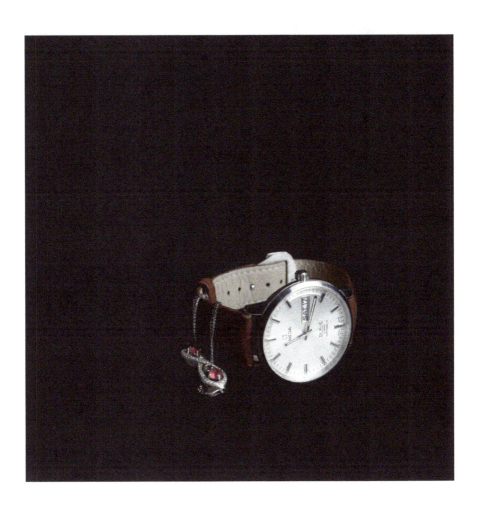

## Alarm clock

A friend in London gave me this alarm clock. I don't even know why I like it. It doesn't remind me of Palestine or my culture, but it does make me think of all the places I've lived. Maybe it symbolizes the process of making friends and a new family in exile.

Academy in Exile Contributors: Exile Things 77

## Torch

My grandfather gave me this torch when I left home. I was only eleven, and he gave it to me so I could find my way in the dark. After the government crackdown in Turkey, I had to leave the country. I took the torch as a memento of my grandfather when he died. He was my favorite person.

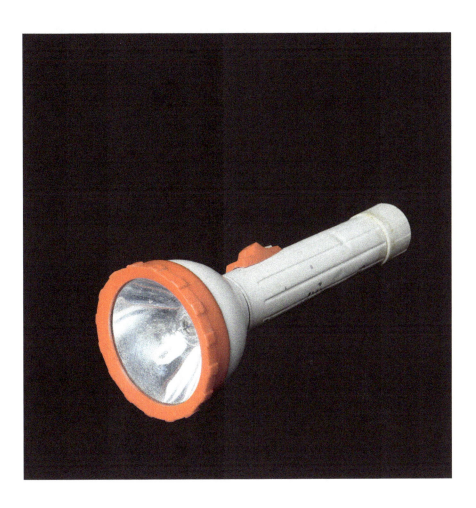

## Ring

I had never thought of leaving my only sister behind. We spent lots of amazing times together, especially shopping, and I got together with her at least once a day. But I have been forced to leave my country and build a life somewhere that is more than three thousand miles away from my sister. I haven't seen her in person in eight years. I brought this ring with me, though. It was her present to remember the good moments that I shared with her back home.

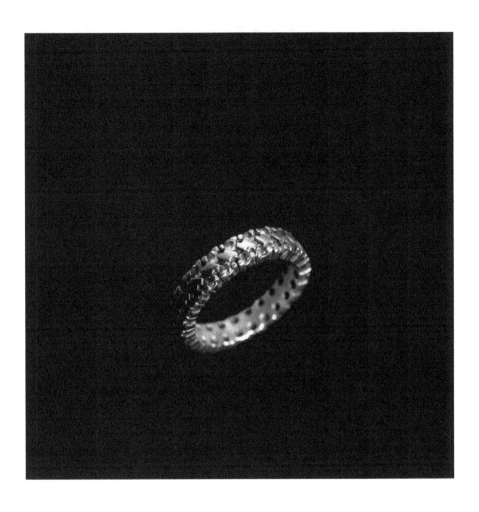

## Necklace

This is my mother's necklace. She inherited it from her mother. My grandmother didn't have enough jewelry to give as wedding presents to each of her five daughters, so she had a goldsmith convert her earrings into two separate necklaces. My mother passed this necklace on to me when I had my daughter. I've always worn it with pleasure, and naturally, I brought it with me when I moved to Germany.

Academy in Exile Contributors: Exile Things 83

## Parting gifts

These were parting gifts from a friend. We met the day before I was scheduled to travel, both of us equally scared of what lay ahead. We somehow wanted to fill each other's absence with small things—a journal which was half written by him, leaving the other pages empty for me to fill.

## Soft little toy

This soft little toy came as a marketing present with something my friend purchased. He knows I get fidgety when I'm anxious, so I need to have something in my hands—something to remind me of the warmth and texture of my *bobas'* (grandmothers') hands—so he gave me the soft toy to hold in case I got anxious.

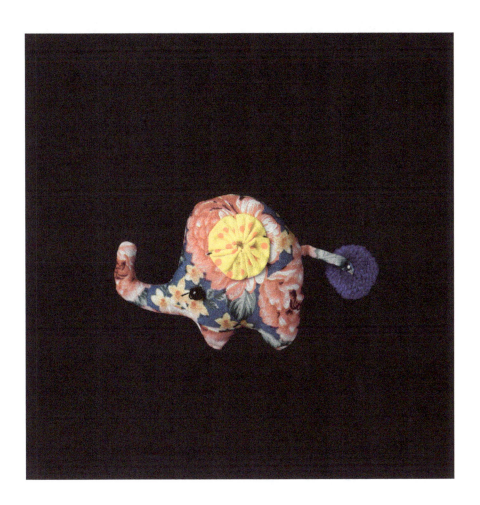

## Postcard

This is a postcard of Khanqah of Shah-e-Hamdan in Kashmir. I belong to Khanqah, everyone says. I was planted there as a child by my father. We made innumerable trips to the old Srinagar city, walking through the narrow alleyways. We spoke of history, food, faith, and love. Khanqah forms a center to my world and my work in myriad ways. My friend knew I would treasure this postcard.

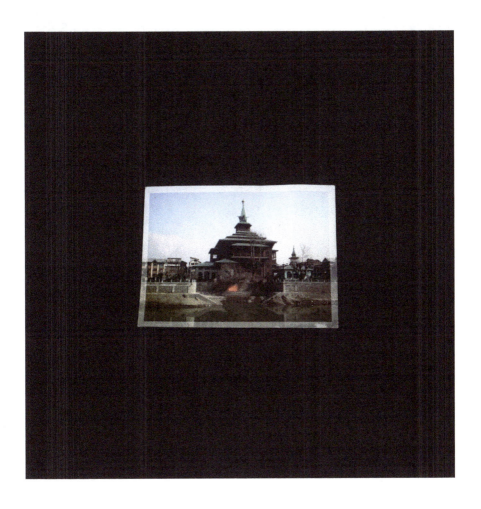

## Fountain pen

This LAMY fountain pen was a birthday gift from a friend to whom I no longer speak. The pen has been a curious witness to so much, knowing more than anyone else. One look at it and nostalgia for obscure things flares up. Forgetfulness does not pull me away, and memory does not draw me in close.

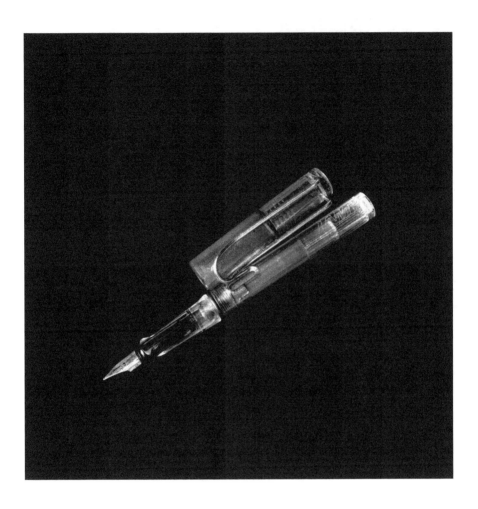

## Letter

This letter is from my teacher, who became a close friend and nurtured me intellectually. On the back is a drawing done by her child. She gave me the letter when I returned after a long absence. Wherever you go in the world, you can find family. I am part of her family. You could say her family is a gift to me from the world.

## Books

When the protests started in Syria, I moved to Delhi. Then Muslims were targeted at the university, and I fled without papers to Jordan. It was hard to choose which books to pack. The day I left for Berlin, it was Edward W. Said's birthday, so I said to myself, "Let me take those." The books used up my luggage allowance. Now my library is scattered around the world.

## Notebooks

A friend gave me one of these notebooks as a present. I brought it with me to Berlin simply because it happened to be the journal I was keeping at the moment. I recall jotting stuff down on the plane without being even dimly aware of the significance that it would later hold for me. The rest of my journals are still in Ankara, lying in a dusty drawer in our apartment. I take some pleasure in thinking of them, their pages yellow and the ink faded, as if they were crafting a quiet place for themselves in Turkey.

## Kitschy photo

When I came to Germany, I planned on staying just five days. Now it's day 1,653 in exile, but who's counting? As a joke, my friend sent me this photo of where I used to live. It's so kitschy. When you look at it, you have to laugh. You can't get emotional.

Academy in Exile Contributors: Exile Things    99

## Pictures of an old man with a cat and a hand-embroidered scarf

These two prints have always decorated my walls in exile. They remind me of my home and the people I miss. The scene of an old man and a cat symbolizes peace, tranquility, and colorfulness in a country associated with conflict, war, and radicalism. The scarf was made by the small hands of internally displaced girls in Kabul to help support their families.

## Oil painting

This oil painting is by a physician-painter whom I met at my parents' house in my hometown during a summer break while I was still working on my doctorate in the United States. The painter gave it to me after an afternoon spent discussing art and literature. I took it with me to the United States, which at that time still seemed a place of no return. A new home. When I returned to Turkey, I took it with me. And in departing for Germany this time, I realized that I had packed it one more time, still unaware of the ways in which I valued it. I did not even have it framed all these years, nor hang it on any wall. I have this stubborn recollection that the painter told me he named the painting "Gathered Beneath the Storm," which of course cannot be true. Yet it's the only name this painting has for me now, a small testament to the power of art and friendship, qualities that possess no home in this world yet make home possible.

## Queer flag

I got this flag from the Jewish section of Gay Pride. I marched joyfully, but fascism is rampant in Poland, and a bill in Parliament goes so far as to actually ban such events. In fact, they are referred to as "Equality Marches." Equality is precisely what my country is lacking right now. Yet the joy of rebuilding Jewish, feminist, and queer Lublin has not been abandoned altogether, nor have I been crushed by persecution at the hands of Poland's minister for education and science. Lublin was once a hub of Jewish, Ukrainian, Protestant, socialist, and atheist thought, and outstanding queer writers went about their work. Just think of lesbian writer Narcyza Żmichowska, author of Gothic novels in the nineteenth century, or Józef Czechowicz, gay poet of the interwar avant-garde! I took this flag with me to Berlin so as to recall the pluralism that is under threat in Poland. I dream of intercultural hospitality returning to my city, my country, the planet.

Academy in Exile Contributors: Exile Things 105

## Keypad phone

This is the phone I brought with me when I left Myanmar last year. I kept it because it's a poignant reminder of life under military rule. After the coup of February 1, 2021, many people, including me, had to buy keypad phones. Most people use smartphones to access the internet and social media, and so switching to keypad phones would not be our choice. We are forced to use them although they have smaller screens and fewer technical features. Using these kinds of phones hasn't really made our lives, which are under constant physical and digital surveillance, that much safer. Popular social media platforms and texting apps like Facebook, WhatsApp, and Messenger are banned and have to be used with virtual private networks (VPNs) that most, if not all, of us once knew nothing about. VPNs are only installed on the smartphones we keep at home. There are many reports of the security forces viewing people carrying keypad phones with suspicion and ordering them to produce the smartphones they actually use.

## Afghan flag

I keep this flag out of a love for my homeland and in memory of the friends and relatives with whom I spent my childhood. After a certain time, it became impossible for us to live together anymore. The flag is just a little piece of home that I took with me when I left. Now it hangs on the wall of my flat in Bonn.

### Venetian silk purse

I thought I might be arrested at the airport in Islamabad. I put my travel documents in this fancy purse and flashed it around at immigration. The officials started whispering to one another, "Why does she keep her things in such an expensive purse?" They barely glanced at my travel documents and escorted me to the VIP lounge for tea while I waited for my flight.

Academy in Exile Contributors: Exile Things 111

## Fur

This is a piece of fur from my dog. I have this one shirt with me that I have never worn since I left the country. One day, I took a closer look at it and saw the fur of my dog on it. I felt that this is the only memory of him that came all the way with me. I put it in a container and kept it with me. I really miss him.

Academy in Exile Contributors: Exile Things   113

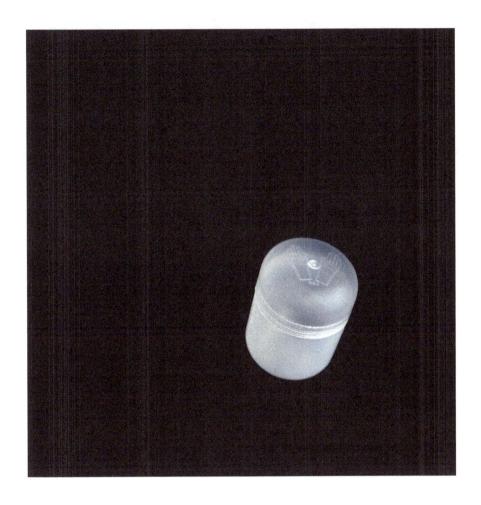

## Coffee cups

I had coffee with a friend I hadn't seen in a long time. We drank from disposable cups, but I kept them anyway. They've traveled with me from country to country. I didn't know if I'd see my friend in two or three years, or ever again, so I preserved these cups. War turns human beings into disposable things.

## Ultrasound

When we set off, this ultrasound was the only object we had that belonged to our unborn daughter. Our journey did not end when we arrived in a safe country, but rather months later when she was born. When we first took her healthy form in our arms, it was only then that we could say, "Here we are." More than for us, this journey was for you, our precious daughter. As a letter from you to us and from us to you, this ultrasound was the only thing that we couldn't leave behind.

Academy in Exile Contributors: Exile Things 117

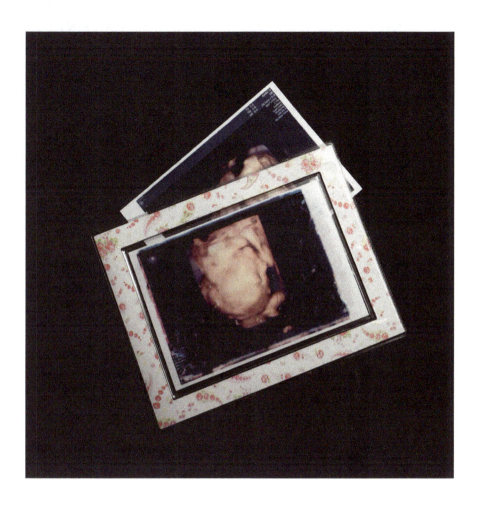

## Toy bear

At the age of six, I became a homeless child. One day during my scavenging, I found this bear on a garbage heap. That was in the late '90s, and from then on, he has accompanied all my steps. He was with me when I left my Roma community, when I obtained my Master's in Media and Communication Studies, when I had my same-sex marriage, and when I defended my doctoral dissertation as well. More than thirty years later, I showed the toy to my husband. Ever since we met, he has called me Miśu, which means "bear" in Polish. It was he who noticed that the bear is sitting on a pile of newspapers. He said, "Miśu, it is you!"

Academy in Exile Contributors: Exile Things 119

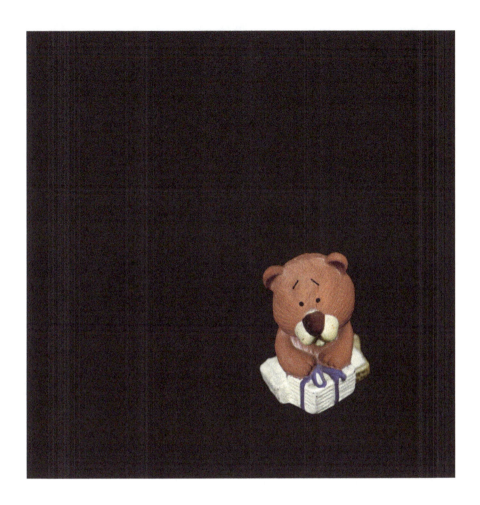

## Green frog

My mother loves to knit. She made this by herself for me. I remember how surprised she was when she saw me really enjoy her gift. I couldn't leave this frog behind, and so I have taken it with me on this journey.

Academy in Exile Contributors: Exile Things    121

## Amber with embedded insects

Whenever I pack my suitcase to move to another country, a country about which I know almost nothing, I toss this necklace into the corner of my bag. It's been there for more than a decade and seen six countries. Am I attached to it? Not really! It neither signifies anything nor even conjures up a particular memory. I only touch it once before departure when I'm packing, and one other time when I arrive at my destination. It has become a banal personal ritual. It serves as a tactile reminder that I've entered a new country and left one more behind. The first time I held it in my hand as a gift, it brought to mind the cruelty of containment. Now it conjures up the state of being always on the move. I like having it, though. It's a constant reminder that home is yet to come and that some people have to move fast enough to stay put.

Academy in Exile Contributors: Exile Things 123

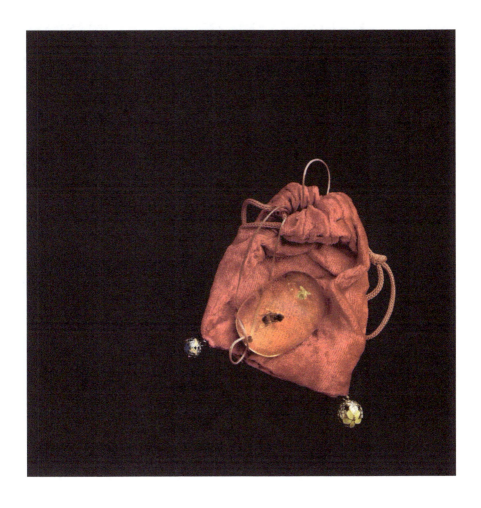

## Amulet

This amulet is called *nazar boncuğu* in Turkish. A friend of mine gave it to me. This is just one of the objects that I carried with me, hoping to be protected on my way to a safer place.

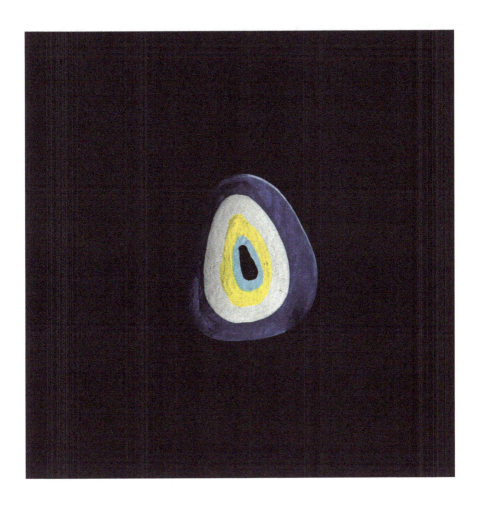

## Keychain

A school friend in Syria gave me this keychain. I hope to return to see him, yet deep inside I know it'll be a long, long journey. The problem is, if you return, you return to someone else, and in the meantime, you, yourself, have become someone else. The object, with all its memories, freezes a moment in time. I cherish all small things that are gifted to me.

Academy in Exile Contributors: Exile Things 127

## Indian misbaha

These were my mother's prayer beads. I got them from her just before parting. She used them to recall God; now I use them to recall her. When you're on the move, you just take what's most precious to you at that moment. You take whatever you can. But you always have the feeling that you should've brought more. That feeling is always there.

## Syrian misbaha

While in India, a friend of mine came to visit. I already owned a set of prayer beads, but she gave me these because she said she never wanted me to forget Syria. The beads are black. That was her choice.

Academy in Exile Contributors: Exile Things 131

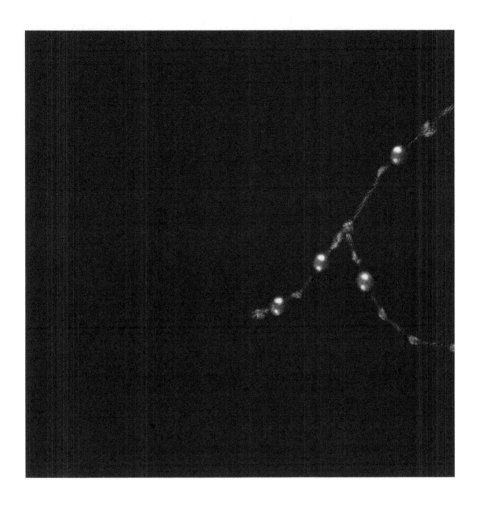

# Art Market as Community Builder: Empowering the Makers of Welcome Editions

*Kate Bonansinga*

Since its founding in 2014 by artists Calgano (Cal) Cullen and Geoffrey (Skip) Cullen, Wave Pool in Cincinnati, Ohio, has commissioned nine internationally recognized artists and dozens of craftspeople, many of them migrants and refugees, to work together to create limited-edition artworks under the imprint of Welcome Editions. Both the artists and the fabricators earn payment up front.[1] Each edition is designed, approved, and signed by the artist. Wave Pool rented a booth at The Armory Show (New York City) in 2021, 2022, and 2023, the Independent Art Fair (New York City) in 2022, and Expo Chicago in 2023; they sold the editions and commanded prices that audiences of such art fairs expect. The proceeds from each edition finance the next one. Thus, Welcome Editions harnesses the exuberance of the fine art market to support both artists and craftspeople, offering a silver lining to the commodification of art. In this chapter, I will illustrate the importance of this action by applying ideas developed by twentieth-century cultural theorists to three Welcome Editions that specifically address displacement and the importance of community, drawing upon the personal experience of the makers to enforce the artistic concept. Throughout, the term migrant refers to a person who moves from one place to another to find better work or living conditions; a refugee is a person who has been forced to leave their country in order to escape persecution.

---

1   Fabricators earn a minimum of $25.00 per hour; some earn more.

Since at least the 1970s, the artistic avant-garde has been resisting art-as-product. Installation art, performance art, and video art are some of the genres that developed at that time because many artists wanted to create a non-object-oriented, temporal experience that could not be bought or sold. In the decades following, several critical theories of culture focused on consumer goods and objects and their role in society. For example, in 1986, Arjun Appadurai's influential edited volume *The Social Life of Things: Commodities in Cultural Perspective* focused "on the things that are exchanged rather than simply on the forms or functions of exchange" (3). In 1999, Graham Harman posited Object Oriented Ontology (OOO), which studies the nature of being by placing the "thing" front and center. Then, in 2001, Bill Brown's "Thing Theory" borrowed from Heidegger's distinction between objects and things and posited that an object becomes a thing when "the insufficiency of the desired object" (2003, 4) becomes clear.[2] We begin to confront the thingness of objects when they stop working for us. In short, cultural and social intellectuals were (and are) trying to make sense of all of the stuff in our lives on the heels of fine artists who resisted, and continue to resist, the production of more material goods and the market that production engenders. Welcome Editions are object-based and collectible, but because one of their goals is social justice for refugees, they turn commodification on its head.

---

2    Brown subsequently reveals his understanding of "art's drive to reify itself and thus resist commodification" (2003, 13).

*Figure 5.1: Lorena Molina, At what cost?, Welcome Edition #8, duotone print, embroidery, walnut frame, 2023, edition of 6, 21"H X 30"W.*

Source: Photograph courtesy of Wave Pool

*Figure 5.2: Lorena Molina, Do you feel safe?, Welcome Edition #8, duotone print, embroidery, walnut frame, 2023, edition of 6, 18"H X 30"W.*

Source: Photograph courtesy of Wave Pool

*Figure 5.3: Lorena Molina,* For who?, *Welcome Edition #8, duotone print, embroidery, walnut frame, 2023, edition of 6, 18"H X 30"W.*

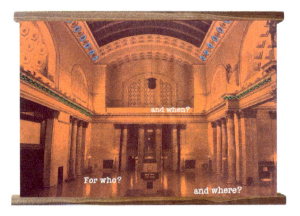

Source: Photograph courtesy of Wave Pool

*Figure 5.4: Lorena Molina,* Do you feel free?, *Welcome Edition #8, duotone print, embroidery, walnut frame, 2023, edition of 6, 18"H X 30"W.*

Source: Photograph courtesy of Wave Pool

## Lorena Molina

Lorena Molina (b. 1985, San Salvador, El Salvador; resides in Houston, Texas), the artist of Welcome Edition #8, was born in El Salvador and lived through the civil war there. In 1999, she and her family migrated to the US to escape the conflict; Molina has grappled with feelings of displacement ever since. Consequently, her artwork focuses on the challenges that immigrants face in establishing new homes and communities. Welcome Edition #8 is a series of four photographs appropriated from internet-based media of sites to which migrants who crossed the southern US border were transported by unwelcoming governors of states such Texas and Florida. The images are of Martha's Vineyard; Vice President Kamala Harris's home near the Naval Observatory in Washington, DC; Chicago's Union Station, and Manhattan's Port Authority (Figs. 5.1 through 5.4). To accompany each one, Molina wrote short phrases such as "Do you feel safe?" "Do you feel free?" and "At what cost?" The artist has iterated these phrases many times before in previous bodies of artwork. These are questions that she is constantly challenging herself and others to ask. How are we complicit in the economic and social exploitation of others?

Molina resides in Houston, Texas, and worked remotely with Cincinnati-based fabricators on Welcome Edition #8. It was the first time that she had worked remotely with a team; she had also never before printed in two tones on fabric, a process that she trusted to University of Cincinnati graduate student Peiyu Liu. Migrant embroiderers associated with Casa de Paz, a Cincinnati-based non-profit that provides safety for Latinas and their children escaping domestic violence, stitched the text on each photograph after receiving Molina's guidance about placement and color. Molina states, "I am constantly thinking about migration, and how you create a place and belonging, and who gets to feel safe and free in this country.... I didn't need to explain the work to [the embroiderers]... they got the concept right away.... I think working with them was the most rewarding part of it" (Zoom interview with author, 14 June 2023). Each piece is partially framed by a strip of wood, one on top and one on the bottom, fabricated by Jake Girth, so that it suspends much like an Asian hanging scroll, though Molina's pieces are wider than they are tall. The presentation format highlights the concept of suspension and instability, of waiting to land. Fabrication by a team supports Molina's interest in community and inclusion; the fabrication process confirms the artistic concept while also offering Molina a method of expanding her capabilities and impact.

*Figure 5.5: Welcome Editions booth at Expo Chicago 2023.*

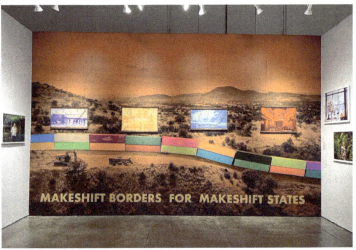

The land border between the US and Mexico is 699 miles long, and much of it is remote desert territory where the physical barrier between the two countries is either nonexistent or permeable, an undefined in-between place. Wave Pool unveiled Welcome Edition #8 at Expo Chicago in 2023. Molina designed a photographic wall mural with an image of the US/Mexico border (specifically a location where the border "wall" is in reality a fence) superimposed with an image of a line of railroad freight cars stacked two high, altered so that their colors are fluorescent. In 2022, Arizona's then-governor began to construct what was to be a ten-mile-long temporary barrier consisting of stacked shipping containers through a federally protected forest on the state's southern border. (The project was illegal and never completed, but it damaged a vital wildlife corridor.) Molina's representation looks like a child's train set or stacking blocks, alluding to the border as a political toy, as well as to "La Bestia," the freight train on top of which Central American migrants ride across Mexico, risking their lives. The four scrolls hung on top of this mural-cum-wallpaper (Fig. 5.5). Molina states, "I was mostly thinking about this idea of makeshift borders, and I wanted that to be the space where the images are seen" (interview, 14 June 2023). This presentation emphasized the point that national borders are political fabrications, rooted in the assertion of ownership and power, and in dividing people from one another.

Brown's Thing Theory might posit that the currency of this message will determine whether Welcome Edition #8 is an object or a thing. As long as there are nation-states with borderlands that are far from the centers of political power, and as long as there are diasporic peoples attempting to create a new home, and as long as someone somewhere is looking at Welcome Edition #8 and being reminded of this political condition, it will be an object that serves its function. (Brown [2003, 3] describes his new idiom as beginning with the effort to think with or through the physical object world.) Object Oriented Ontology (Harman 1999) might suggest that in the case of Welcome Edition #8, the idea itself, rather than the physical object that conveys it, is the thing. The idea is front and center.

## Baseera Khan

Baseera Khan (b. 1980, Denton, Texas; resides in Brooklyn, New York) grew up in Texas, the child of working-class Muslim parents who migrated from Bangalore, India. The family lived in near isolation due to the threat of deportation; much of Khan's artwork references displacement and the Muslim experience in the US. Khan's Welcome Edition #7 is a prayer rug emblazoned with the verbiage "Muslims = America" to remind us that the US was and continues to be built on the physical and intellectual labor of many under-recognized peoples (Fig. 5.6) The residue of the political backlash from 11 September 2001, when al-Qaeda terrorists crashed planes into the twin towers of the World Trade Center in New York City, remains in the American psyche. The misplaced identification of Muslims as terrorists is a component of that residue. Khan reminds us that the stereotype is misplaced.

*Figure 5.6: Baseera Khan,* Muslims=America, Welcome Edition #7, *wool, 2022, edition of 13, 36"H X 24"W.*

It began as a protest poster: seven letters in each word make the equation true. When approached by Wave Pool to create an edition, Khan decided that the message would translate well into a woven and embroidered prayer rug, and that it would be further empowered by a material and format that refers to the expression of worship, woven by female refugees from Central Asia, specifically Bhutan, who lived and wove in refugee camps in Nepal before coming to the US.[3] Muslims are only one of the possible population groups to identify in the piece. Khan implies that we could and should imagine the insertion of other marginalized groups in lieu of "Muslims": women, African Americans, Asian Americans, LGBTQIA peoples, etc. Khan shares, "Yes, there are complexities with race, class, gender, but at the end of the day, there is a very central human instinct.... We have to come together collectively to achieve those goals" (Zoom interview with author, 26 June 2023).

Contemporary Arts Center in Cincinnati hosted Khan's solo exhibition *Weight on History*, and through this the artist became familiar with the city. Several rugs exhibited there were designed by Khan and fabricated by craftspeople in Kashmir. Khan shares, "I think that my work becomes more powerful because of the moves that I make actually relying on a community of craftspeople." Speaking about Welcome Edition #7 and the Bhutanese weavers, Khan states that it was "important for me to work with this particular group during this time of rising xenophobia and fascism all over this country and all over the world.... [it was] a process of me wanting a particular design and them coming back to me and saying, well, we can't do this ... but we can do this, or we don't have this color, but we have this. It was a generative collaboration." Khan was also motivated by the fact that the weavers would benefit financially. "Money is a funny thing. It means everything but nothing at the same time" (interview, 26 June 2023).

---

3   Ethnic Nepalese were forced out of Bhutan in the 1990s to refugee camps in Nepal. By 2016 most of the Bhutanese refugees had been resettled in the US. Cincinnati received many of them. https://www.wgbh.org/news/2016/12/29/bhutanese-refugee-camps-nepal-wind-down-resettlement-program-considered-success.

Khan seems interested in the mercilessness of financial markets and in questioning who benefits from the art market. For example, in the exhibition "iamuslima," Khan's New York debut in 2017, the print *Prayer (prostrating in submission five times a day to an entity outside of your body)* included the lines "SOME FAMILIES STACK THE DOLLAR BILLS. MY FAMILY STACKS THE TRAUMA. NOW I'M TRYING TO MAKE SOME MONEY OFF UNDERSTANDING MY MAMA'S DRAMA" (Larmon 2017, 364). Another, less direct example is Khan's *The Liberator* (2022), a 3-D acrylic bust rendered from a digital scan of Khan's own body sliced at chakra points.[4] It was inspired by Naro Dakini, a ferocious female Tibetan Buddhist deity who wears a garland of skulls and a skirt of bones, an eighteenth-century example of which is in the collection of the National Museum of Asian Art (Smithsonian Institution 2023). By referencing the historical sculpture, Khan also challenges us to question the appropriateness of the museum display of a religious object intended for Buddhist devotion and prayer. Other questions expand from this one: How did this object come to the US? Who gained and who lost in this transaction? The market probably determined its monetary value and dismissed its cultural one when it was extracted from its home and its original purpose. Who was complicit in the financial transaction does not matter as much as acknowledging that we are all complicit now.

*The Liberator*'s iconography illustrates blockages of feminine power; its historical reference conveys our responsibility to interpret and understand the beliefs of those from places and times other than our own, manifesting Appadurai's (1986) goal of lending new perspectives on the circulation of commodities in social life. What was originally an object of Tibetan Buddhist devotion became a commodity the moment it was sold to a Western collector. Later, when it was accessioned into the collection of an art museum, it transformed for the second time, into a work of art. Brown (2003, 46) confirms that physical objects have metaphysical properties. Those properties of this object changed as it moved across international borders and into a museum setting. Wave Pool capitalizes

---

4  Chakra means "wheel" in Sanskrit and refers to energy points in the body.

on the market that Khan and Brown critique, bringing social justice to the crass commerce of the global art fair.

## Vanessa German

"If you could make a piece of art that had a superpower, what would it be?" artist Vanessa German (b. 1976, Milwaukee, Wisconsin; resides in Pittsburgh, Pennsylvania) asked attendees of the first workshop for Welcome Edition #6. After hearing the answers, German developed a plan for creating the multiple parts that would comprise each of the eleven Power Figures in the edition. The components, all blue, include carved wood torsos by Nigerian wood carver Michael Olludare; cast ceramic songbirds and anatomical hearts by two members of Visionaries and Voices, an organization that supports alternatively gifted makers; and woven and dyed fabric shaped like teardrops or water, with a wish for the future handwritten by workshop participants and other community members encased inside each one. German guided twelve to fifteen helpers in the assemblage of each sculpture and then completed each one with additional parts and marks. "Her hands are like magic," states Cal Cullen, artist, co-founder of Wave Pool, and director of Welcome Editions. "This blue is like a feeling, it is a powerful emotion. She keeps coming back to this color again and again" (interview with author, Cincinnati, Ohio, 26 June 2023). Titled *a holy blue togetherness for planetary awareness of the single universal breath*, the edition exemplifies, in German's words, "how the color blue is a gift; for the gifts of water, creativity, and togetherness as balm and center in times of disconnect and delusion: a way to be here together. A way of loving" (Fig. 5.7).[5]

---

5   https://www.wavepoolgallery.org/welcomeeditions.

*Figure 5.7: Vanessa German,* a holy blue togetherness for planetary awareness of the single universal breath, *Welcome Edition #6 (front), mixed media, 2022, edition of 10, approximately 15"H X 12"W X 10"D.*

German's overall efforts as an artist focus on collective healing from systemic racism; by honestly admitting the injustices of the past, we can correct our present behaviors and look toward a better future. Her sculptures are generous in their physical and visual abundance. She is munificent in her daily life as well. In 2011, she founded Love Front Porch to provide a time and space for her neighbors in Pittsburgh to create and share. (This enterprise grew into ARThouse, a community studio, artist's residency, and outdoor theater and garden.) In each of her assembled sculptures, she brings together disparate objects to build a cohesive expression, much as she coalesces individuals to make a community.

Sometimes, German uses articles from everyday life and repurposes them as components for her sculptures, a quintessential example of transforming dysfunctional things into meaningful objects if we apply Brown's Thing Theory. But for Welcome Edition #6, each of the individual components was fabricated anew by skilled craftspeople: a glass blower, a wood carver, a ceramist, and several weavers, among others, participated in this community effort. German combines lovingly crafted objects into another object that has even greater meaning because of her input: theorizing through OOO, the being of the thing is multiplied. Cal Cullen, who hand-built one of the ceramic components, describes, "A lot of it was about connecting people, about creating inclusive spaces, being able to lift one another up" (interview, 26 June 2023).

In its review of the Independent Art Fair 2022, the *New York Times* mentioned only a few artists; German (presented by Wave Pool and Kasmin) was one of them (Heinrich 2022). Maria Seda-Reder, Director of Exhibitions/Artist Support Initiatives at Wave Pool, staffed Wave Pool's booth at the fair. She recalls, "We are leveraging the names and cultural cachet of really important artists on behalf of the local community.... For some people, that really resonated: collectors, curators, gallerists... people who themselves are artists... [are] searching for more meaning in art-making. It is so important right now" (interview with author, Cincinnati, Ohio, 28 June 2023).

Wave Pool and German have similar motivations and working methods: both bring people together to generate meaning for the makers and the audience alike, and sometimes these two groups are one and the same. This type of art making has been ascending in importance since the beginning of the twenty-first century. Generally known as socially engaged art, it is rooted in Nicholas Bourriaud's *Relational Aesthetics*. It blurs the divide between artist and audience as a method for empowering the latter to be an agent of change. "The role of artworks is... to actually be ways of living and models of action..." (Bourriaud 2002, 13).

This builds on the previously mentioned artistic resistance of the 1970s against the commodification of art. Wave Pool claims socially engaged art as one of its institutional foci, making the creation, marketing, and sale of its Welcome Editions a socially engaged practice. The institution itself is a socially engaged practitioner.[6]

## Conclusion

Other Welcome Editions gain resonance because they are fabricated by migrants and refugees. For example, Jeffrey Gibson's (b. 1972, Colorado Springs, Colorado; resides in Hudson, New York) Welcome Edition #5 comprises twenty-five weavings, each about the size of a notebook page, with the text "Let Me Be Who You Need Me to Be" as the main image (Fig. 5.8). Gibson is Choctaw/Cherokee and much of his work is abstract, but this one, executed in patterns and colors found in much traditional Native American art, speaks directly to the egregious displacement of Native Americans by the US government. Robbed of land and dignity, they were forced to assimilate. Welcome Edition #5 was woven by refugees from Nepal and Togo who are finding a new home in the US and who likely identify with Gibson's message that the responsibility of adaptation and acceptance is shared by those who have migrated and those who have not—or, more expansively, by anyone in any type of relationship with any other being. Gibson chose to leave each weaving attached to its wooden loom, which in turn serves as its frame, a reminder of the making process and of one of the artworks' messages: change and movement are constant. Guillermo Galindo's soon-to-be-realized edition will be built from things left behind by migrants near the US/Mexico border.

---

6  Wave Pool is an example of New Institutionalism, which refers to "critically reflexive work... that emerged in the 1990s... to redefine the contemporary art institution and its role in expanded notions of the exhibition and social engagement" (Voorhies 2017, 17).

Kate Bonansinga: Art Market as Community Builder    147

*Figure 5.8: Jeffrey Gibson,* Let Me Be Who You Need Me to Be, Welcome Edition #5, *8/2 Tencel weft with a cotton warp, cherry finished pieces are 17"W x 21"H X 17"W.*

Each of these Welcome Editions supports Wave Pool's mission as "a socially engaged art center that acts as a conduit for community change through artist opportunities and support."[7] Fabrication by migrant

---

7    https://www.wavepoolgallery.org/mission.

makers enforces each Edition's conceptual focus on displacement and the longing for human connection. The iteration of this idea, coupled with the sales proceeds supporting the makers who execute them, many of whom are migrants and refugees, means that Welcome Editions are an effective method for fulfilling Wave Pool's mission. Their commodification lends itself to the theoretical analyses of things and commerce, and also fosters social justice.

## References

Appadurai, Arjun. 1986. *The Social Life of Things: Commodities in Cultural Perspective*. Cambridge: Cambridge University Press.

Bourriaud, Nicolas. 2002. *Relational Aesthetics*. Translated by Simon Pleasance and Fronza Woods Dijon: Les Presses du réel.

Brown, Bill. 2003. *A Sense of Things: The Object Matter of American Literature*. Chicago: University of Chicago Press.

Harman, Graham. 1999. "Tool-Being: Elements in a Theory of Objects." PhD diss., DePaul University, 1999.

Heinrich, Will. 2022. "An Elegant Return to Form at Independent Art Fair." *The New York Times*, 5 May. https://www.nytimes.com/2022/05/05/arts/design/independent-art-fair-new-york-review.html.

Larmon, Annie Godfrey. 2017. "Baseera Khan: Participant Inc." *Artforum International Magazine*, 30 November. https://www.artforum.com/print/reviews/201706/baseera-khan-68726.

Smithsonian Institution. 2023. "Baseera Khan: The Liberator, May 04–Jul 16, 2023." *Hirshhorn Museum and Sculpture Garden | Smithsonian*, 16 July. https://hirshhorn.si.edu/exhibitions/baseera-khan-the-liberator/.

Voorhies, James Timothy. 2017. *Beyond Objecthood: The Exhibition as a Critical Form Since 1968*. Cambridge, MA: The MIT Press.

# Amy Conger's Double Exile

*Amy Lind*

This story is still in the making, after so many years. My aunt Amy Conger died in March 2023. Following her passing, I traveled to Santiago in May to meet some of her friends from the time she lived in Chile. I brought with me some of her ashes, to leave in her beloved adopted home. It was a life-changing moment for me, as I came to learn so much more about Amy and was able to confirm much of what I had suspected but which she had never directly told me.[1]

Amy died fifty years after the brutal military coup in Chile, which ultimately affected approximately thirty thousand people through execution, detention, torture, and/or forced exile during the Chilean military regime's seventeen years in power (1973–90). In 1974, one year after the 11 September 1973 military coup, Amy was detained, held at the notorious

---

1   I called Amy my "aunt" although she was really a cousin. She was my mother's first cousin, and as I didn't have any aunts or uncles of my own, she became my "aunt." There is a tradition of Amy Congers in my family; in my case, Conger is my middle name. I am very grateful to the people I have met who knew Amy and who have helped me put together the pieces of her experience. In particular, I want to thank Carlos Torres for sharing stories of Amy's life in Santiago, and for showing me memorialized and unmarked places/spaces where Amy spent time. Indeed, my time spent in Santiago in May 2023 was invaluable. I also want to thank Lynnie Westafer for sharing her knowledge and stories, including the extensive in-person interviews she conducted with Amy in early 2023. I could not have compiled this history without her help and support. I also thank Amy's dear friends from Santiago, including Silvia, Dago, Patricio, and Yvonne, and her dear friends from Riverside, California, especially Jane Carney and Rob McMurray.

War Academy of the Chilean Air Force (Academia de Guerra de la Fuerza Áerea de Chile, or FACH) detention center, and tortured by the Chilean military while living and working as a photographer and art history professor at the Universidad de Chile in Santiago (1971–74).

In fact, Amy was more fortunate than many. While she was detained, she was forced to sign a statement claiming that she was a traitor to Chile, her adopted home, but as a foreigner and US American, she was released thirteen days after her detention in October 1974 and expelled from Chile. Most Chileans were detained for much longer; many never reappeared. Their "disappearance"[2] became essentially permanent, although some family members and activists continue to refer to them as disappeared rather than proclaim them dead. This is in part because their remains were never found, and in part because their loved ones refuse to end a chapter of history that post-dictatorship governments have often tried to conclude or forget.

Amy survived. She returned to the United States, where she immediately began advocating for herself and on behalf of Chileans, whom she viewed as victims of the military dictatorship. Through her public advocacy, she became a political pawn once again, this time in the context of Cold War politics and US foreign policy. She was politically savvy and incredibly strong. Contacting other US Americans who had been detained by the Chilean military, she entreated her contacts to help her tell her story to the media. It all happened fairly quickly: in late 1984 and 1985, she appeared on the national network NBC's *The Today Show* with Barbara Walters and on historian and broadcaster Studs Terkel's radio show.[3] Liberal *Washington Post* journalist Jack Anderson (1974; 1975a) wrote about

---

2   It was due to the wave of military authoritarianism in Latin America in the 1960s through the 1980s that "to disappear" became a verb. As people were "disappeared," with no trace of their whereabouts, the concept has become a standard part of many languages. In the *Merriam-Webster Dictionary*, for example, "to disappear" means "to cause (someone or something) to disappear; a) to abduct and kill or imprison (someone, such as a political dissident) while withholding information about the person's fate"; https://www.merriam-webster.com/dictionary/disappear.

3   I do not have access to a copy of the *Today Show* segment.

her case, arguing that Amy was a victim of US foreign policy in Chile. His conservative counterpart William F. Buckley, in turn, published op-eds in the *Post* rebuking Anderson's claims. He referred to Amy as an American communist who was suspected by the Chilean Intelligence "of being Mata Hari" and who deserved to be detained (1974).

Importantly, in 1975, Amy joined a group of US citizens, including Terkel, who filed a lawsuit against the US Department of State, including against then–Secretary of State Henry Kissinger, charging the US government with crimes against humanity for their support of the overthrow and assassination of democratically elected President Salvador Allende and the subsequent Chilean military coup. She testified to the US Congress about her experience of detention (Kennedy 1974). Unsurprisingly, they did not "win" their lawsuit. The lawsuit did, however, help block additional funding for Chile that the Senate was then voting upon.[4] For a short time, her story symbolized the strong ideological Cold War divide within the United States, including the fear of Cuba's "domino effect" in the region; that is, the fear that communism would spread throughout Latin America and threaten US democracy.

Through all of this, I now know, Amy suffered. When I was young, I remember watching her on *The Today Show* and thinking what a strong, impressive person she was. Amy rarely talked about how she felt about her experience, but for years she feared retaliation while living in the United States. I first interviewed her in 1984, while still a college student. I visited my older and much admired relative at her brother's house in Los Angeles, and we talked at length. She told me about the years after

---

4   As Amy Conger states in a draft letter she prepared on 11 February 1975 to share with multiple US political leaders, "On December 4, 1974, Sen. Kennedy presented an amendment to the Foreign Assistance Act of 1974 to cut off all military aid to Chile because of the terrible violations of Human Rights which are presenting occurring there.... This bill was passed as amended in the Senate and subsequently in the House of Representatives where, additionally, the total amount of economic aid was diminished from approximately $60 million to $25 million for the same reason." Following Jack Anderson's story about Amy's case, Amy's testimony to the US Congress, and the group lawsuit, the US government significantly cut funds to Chile. See also Anderson (1975b).

her return to the US and her worry about being followed. She adopted a German Shepherd as a form of protection, and she made sure she had a network of friends in her local community who kept an eye out for her and helped support her. Once, when she traveled to Mexico City to give a talk about her experience in Chile at an Amnesty International conference, she recognized a US American intelligence agent outside her hotel room. She heard someone fumbling with keys and trying to get into her room so she barricaded the door with a large piece of furniture. She was eventually able to leave and asked people from Amnesty International to move her to another hotel. She believed the intelligence agent wanted to assassinate her. This fear of being persecuted never dissipated. In an interview Amy gave to a journalist family friend in early 2023, she said she never stopped looking in the rearview mirror of her car even then, forty-nine years after her initial detention in Chile.[5]

Amy was forcibly exiled from Chile, but she was displaced in her own country as well upon her return. She was blacklisted, and for several years, she faced difficulties finding a job, including as a professor. In Chile, she had witnessed atrocities that her own government had helped manufacture. She made an intentional decision to stay and join the wide range of Chileans who resisted military disappearances, detentions, torture, and executions. She was a strong believer in human rights and enamored by Chile's democratic socialism. She joined the resistance, which, at the time, included anyone opposed to military rule. In her case, she worked with MIR (Movimiento de Izquierda Revolucionaria, or Revolutionary Left Movement), a movement to the left of Allende's socialism that supported the Allende administration, worked toward the redistribution of wealth, and opposed US and other forms of western/northern imperialism. MIR was one of the most repressed political movements by the military junta; many MIR members were victims of state violence, although it was also a relatively resilient movement (Amat 2023). Once Amy began to witness the military repression, she made a conscious decision to remain in Santiago and work with

---

5   Interview with Amy Conger by Lynnie Westafer; personal communication with Lynnie Westafer, 14 July 2023.

others to resist military and state violence. She continued to work at the Universidad de Chile, which was taken over by the military soon after the coup. Almost all professors at the university were fired. Amy was one of eight professors who remained on staff, perhaps because the military initially believed a US American would be a safe person to have on staff, perhaps even an ally. And yet, in September 1974, a year after the military coup, Amy was detained in front of her house, bringing her resistance to a halt. She was handcuffed, blindfolded, and forced to walk from her house to the military vehicle with her shirt raised over her head, a common practice by the military to humiliate and dehumanize people, often in the view of bystanders. After her detention, she was deported and then forced into an "inner emigration," a kind of exile within her own country.

It is very possible that her photographs of Chile in the early 1970s were one factor leading to her arrest and detention. Indeed, her photos powerfully reflect the revolutionary fervor of the time. The photo included here ("Untitled"), of a young child drinking milk—benefiting from President Allende's milk distribution program in poor neighborhoods—has been widely circulated in Chile and particularly in social media during the past few years. She is rarely credited for the photo despite the fact that it has come to represent a key historical moment and reflects a sentiment of hope that is alive in the national memory today.

Amy did not publish many of the photos she took in Chile until about twenty years later, after the dictatorship fell and it was safe to publish photos of people who may have been retaliated against by the military had they been identified. When Amy was detained at her home in the Bellavista neighborhood in Santiago, she hid many of her photos in her oven so the officers who detained her could not find them. Some were damaged, others were smuggled out of the country, yet others she was able to keep and restore.

154   What We Brought with Us

*Figure 6.1: Amy Conger,* Untitled.

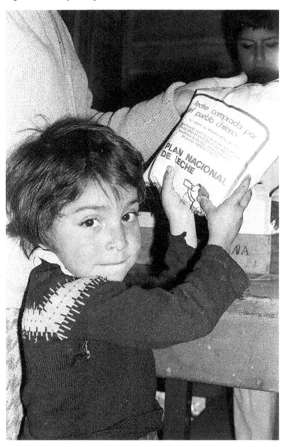

Source: Amy Conger, *Bienvenido to Nueva Havana: Santiago, Chile 1972–1973*. Telluride, CO: Nolvido Press, 2010

In many ways, Amy protected me from her history. She didn't tell me about her involvement in MIR. But putting the pieces together, in retrospect, I see how she carried the memories with her, even though she compartmentalized that experience as a way to survive and also possibly to protect those around her. Her dog Lumi was named after a well-known female leader in MIR, and a friend and comrade of Amy at the time, who was executed by the Chilean military. Amy's forced displacement remained with her for the rest of her life, even though few people around her, including her own family and some friends, really understood what she had experienced, been part of, and witnessed.

When Amy died, she left her possessions to friends of hers from all walks of life. What was most important to her was her art, her photography, her books, her writing and publishing (she published several books on photography and was working on a book on her extensive Chilean *arpillera* collection when she died), and her friends.[6] She had lifelong friendships with her Chilean friends from the early 1970s. She returned to Chile two or three times after the dictatorship ended, where she saw old friends, some of whom had also been detained, tortured, and exiled. She remained close to the grown children of her close comrades who were orphaned following the execution of their parents. She communicated regularly with a Chilean friend who now lives in Mexico City, another who now lives in Buenos Aires, and another in Quito, Ecuador, remaining close to them until she died. After having collectively gone through such a traumatic experience, this group of friends and adopted family was forever bonded. I felt this myself when I met her friends this year.

I found out Amy had died when I was at a conference in Quito. I opened Facebook during a break in my hotel room and saw a photo of Amy posted by a former Chilean graduate student of mine at FLACSO-Ecuador who had returned to Chile to live. She posted the image of Amy as a way to acknowledge the many untold histories of people who suffered from the military dictatorship. It's amazing how memory is retold through social media in such powerful ways. This year (2023), a half

---

6   *Arpilleras* are a type of folk art created largely by women in Chile to document the political violence at a time when assembling in groups of more than two people was not allowed, according to military law. As a result, *arpilleras* have become a powerful source of storytelling and memory surrounding human rights abuses in Chile.

century after the coup, there have been many commemorative events acknowledging those who were executed or disappeared and sharing stories, such as this one about my aunt, with Chilean publics. I cried in my hotel room as I prepared to give a talk about contemporary right-wing attacks on "gender ideology" at the conference.

This photo of the young child drinking milk is emblematic of the much broader historical moment Amy captured in her photography from 1971 to 1974. She captured the soul of a nation hopeful for better lives for the majority, not just for the privileged few. More than her material possessions, Amy loved her photos—and photos in general—that capture the affective dimensions of people's lives, suffering, and care.

Amy Conger's legacy will continue. In bringing some of her ashes to Santiago, I brought part of her home to her adopted home. With the help of a dear friend of hers, her ashes will be placed in the MIR Memorial Mausoleum at the General Cemetery in Santiago. Perhaps ironically, it is easier to talk about her story now than it was when she was alive. This, then, is just the beginning of a much longer story in the making. I will continue to learn from her as my ancestor. And she will guide me and many others as we continue to navigate politics, seek forms of repair, and imagine a more just future.

## References

Amat, Consuelo. 2023. "State Repression and Opposition Survival in Pinochet's Chile." *Comparative Political Studies*. Prepublished 29 May 2023. https://doi.org/10.1177/00104140231169033.
Anderson, Jack. 1974. "U.S. Woman Details Chile Torture." *Washington Post*, 27 November 1974.
Anderson, Jack. 1975a. "Answering Bill Buckley." *New York Post*, 3 January 1975.
Anderson, Jack. 1975b. "Respecting the Torturers in Chile." *Washington Post*, 11 January 1975.
Buckley, William F. Jr. 1974. "Playing with Fire." On the Right, *Washington Post*, 27 November 1974.

Kennedy, Edward. 1974. Senator Kennedy of Massachusetts on Chile military aid cutoff. 93rd Cong., 2nd sess. *Cong. Rec.*, 4 December, vol. 120, pt. 28, 38139–40.

*Studs Terkel Program, The*. 1975. "Amy Conger, Arthur Warner, and Natalie Warner Discuss Chile and the Coup d'Etat in 1973," 20 October 1975. https://studsterkel.wfmt.com/programs/amy-conger-arthur-warner-and-natalie-warner-discuss-chile-and-coup-detat-1973.

# What Matters to Boatpeople: Shirts, Spoons, and Sleep

*Kim Huynh*

*My family left Vietnam by boat in April 1979 with a small bag of possessions and $400 USD hidden in the seams of our clothes.*

*What follows is my translation of conversations in Vietnamese that I had with my parents about what remains from our journey—in particular, a shirt and spoon.*

*As with many items, their value is linked to the history and symbolism we assign to them.*

*While my mother's recollections seem detailed and clear, my father's memory has been affected by sustained hardship, two strokes, Alzheimer's disease, and chronic insomnia.*

*Together, Mum and Dad offer insights into what matters to boatpeople and non-boatpeople alike.*

*When did you last sleep through the night, Dad?*
I have no idea.

I asked your mother, and she can't remember either. She suggested the night our boat reached that tiny island without a name. We were exhausted and fell asleep on the beach. But even then, I recall lying on the sand and peering into the night sky as I tried to figure out what to do next.

What I do know is that since we've been in Australia, I've hardly ever slept for more than four hours straight.

160   What We Brought with Us

*Figure 7.1: The Huynh family, 1975.*

Source: The author's family archive.

I've tried acupuncture, sleep specialists, laboratory studies, meditation, yoga, herbal remedies, those whirring sleep apnea machines. None of them have helped.

I'm ashamed to say that I'm in the habit of taking half a sleeping tablet before bed. Sometimes, I need a full one.

*That's very frustrating for you, isn't it?*
Of course. For almost half a century I've been telling myself, "You can get on top of this."

I'm very strong-willed. Maybe that's the problem.

Every morning, I swim fourteen laps. When I can't get to the pool because my heart's acting up, then I walk up and down the lounge room. If I don't tire myself out in the day, I'll pay for it at night.

Often, I remind myself that I'm a well-educated man of reason, and some accomplishment. I know that all I have to do is nothing. But when the sun sets, I lose my senses.

The doctor says I'm "sundowning." That's why I get so frightened and confused. She's probably right. But isn't everyone prone to "sundowning"? Don't we all crave the fresh hope that morning brings?

When I was little, we used to say that day and night were like *xoi dau*, sticky rice and dried beans. Rice is warm and soft, while beans are hard and unforgiving. I learned that darkness also means chaos and terror. That's when the Viet Minh revolutionaries *di ve* ("came home") from the jungles into the villages. And with them would be gunfire and mortars. I remember the thump of the mortars, "AHM! AHM! AHM!" and being thrust into shelters in the ground.

The Viet Minh used to say that the people were the water that sustained them and through which they moved like fish. But their real water was the darkness. I should know. When I was twelve, I learned to swim with them.

*What do you think about at night?*
The other day, as I fell in and out of a daytime nap, I saw the mountains that loomed over my village.

For us, the mountains were the edge of the world, even though they were only a few kilometers away. Quang Nam province was wedged between the mountains to the west and the East Sea. In fact, instead of using "west" or "east," we'd say "Head down river and turn towards the mountains," or "Take this bushel of rice to the market stall that faces the sea." That's how quaint life was.

Other memories from Vietnam are not so quaint. You'd think that with my Alzheimer's, some of them would fade. But if anything, the scenes from my past have become more vivid as I "approach one hundred years," which is what we Vietnamese say instead of "kicking the bucket."

Sometimes, I see my father. I was only six or seven when he was killed during the war against the French. "Assassinated" is a better word. Your grandmother told me that his hands were tied behind his back when the Viet Minh kicked him into a shallow grave. He called out to relatives and friends who were highly ranked revolutionaries, there to witness his sham trial. None of them helped.

I don't recall his face, yet my father haunts me in his absence. Unlike most Vietnamese, I don't believe in ghosts. But my father, or my memory of him, comes close.

My brother Nho's face I remember very well. Your grandmother said that Nho resembled my father—and that you, my son, resemble Nho.

Your uncle died in the jungle, fighting for the Republic of Vietnam, a few days after his daughter was born. Like me, when he was a teenager he supported the Viet Minh, but soon came to realize that Ho Chi Minh and the communists were ruthless liars.

With Nho's death came waves of grief and resentment. It confirmed in my mind that there's no justice or cosmic force looking out for us.

For your grandmother, tragedy fueled superstition. She could not accept that Nho was gone. And when she finally did, she became obsessed with finding his body and laying his soul to rest. She spent money that we didn't have on fortune tellers and soothsayers, all of them scammers who sent us trekking into the jungle looking for remains that could have belonged to anyone or anything. Looking back, that only made it harder for me to come to grips with my brother's passing.

*Is that when your insomnia started?*
No. I slept fine during the French and American wars.

It was afterwards, when I was planning our escape, that I began to *mat ngu* ("lose sleep").

You know what it's like before you go on a big trip. How you feel the night of an important exam or job interview. You're a father now, so you've experienced the incredible anticipation that builds up when your wife's pregnant. Well, escaping your homeland is like all those things combined, but far more uncertain, intense, and frightening.

Lots of people were leaving. There was a saying at the time, "If light posts could walk, they would go too." Everyone was suspicious of everyone else. A neighbor could tell the local authorities about our suspicious behavior. Someone at work could report us to gain favor with those higher up. An innocent rumor could ruin everything. The pressure was immense.

First, we organized our own small boat in 1978 with another family. But we were swindled and lost our savings. There was no backup plan. We had almost lost hope.

Then, at the start of 1979, your mother's cousin confided in her that she had found a way out for her children. It was with a Chinese syndicate. They would have fake papers saying that they were Chinese-Vietnamese. Due to conflict in the region, the government was eager to get rid of the Chinese, while confiscating their property and wealth.

We didn't have the money to go with them. But despite not wanting us to leave, your grandmother came to the rescue, giving us just enough for the trip. With that, our hope was reignited, but so too was the stress and anticipation.

But I'll let you in on a secret. It was thrilling too. How could it not be? To have a chance of a new beginning after so many dead ends. To risk everything for my family's future.

So with all the fear and dread of getting caught, while trying my best to stay stable amidst the tumult, I started to lose sleep.

Often, I crept out of bed to not disturb your mother, and took out a compass and map that I bought on the black market. In secret, I calculated the routes and distances that our boat might take from oppression to freedom, to a new place to call "home."

*What was it like on the boat?*
The KG-1170. There's a number I'll never forget. Even more important is 392, because we were the 392nd boat to reach Palau Bidong in Malaysia.

That's how they called us up for rations, mail, and for that all-important resettlement interview. "Thiet Van Huynh from Boat 392!"

There's another memorable number, 507. That's how many people were on our twenty-meter boat.

I sat at the front with your brother, sweating and entwined on the deck. It was worse for the young men who were shoved into the hull. Your cousin was down there, not far from the clanking engine. He didn't know whether he was more desperate for water or air. They had to be locked in to ensure that they didn't rush on deck and scuttle the boat. The locked latch was near where your brother and I sat. I can still hear the thumping and hollering from below.

You once asked whether I cried on the boat. I said "never." I don't think any of the adults cried. We were too worried.

*Did you see Mum and me on the boat?*
Yes. You and your mother were in the cabin because you were so small and sick.

Amazingly, your mother found a way to visit us. It was after a couple of days, when the storms had passed and the ocean was calm. We had not eaten anything since leaving and, like everyone around us, had been seasick. Your brother and I were famished.

It was even more amazing that your mum brought us food. She had shimmied around the edge of the boat, with you and a bowl of rice soup in one arm, while holding on to the railing on the outside of the cabin with the other. Note that there was nothing but the Gulf of Thailand below her, and your mother could not swim, not even a meter.

But when she appeared standing over us, the sunshine framing her silhouette, with you and the soup in hand, I did not question the risk she had taken. I just accepted the reward, most of which I gave to your brother, saving a mouthful for myself.

I assumed you and your mother had had some soup too. But she said that you would not eat. You were so weak, lying still in her arms wearing that yellow shirt. Your brother's shirt was in good condition. It had been washed by the rain and dried in the sun. Yours was awfully stained, not with blood but with the medicines, carrots, betel nut, everything that we could find that might give you a chance to live. All of it, you spewed and shat out.

*Figure 7.2: The shirt that Kim Huynh wore when he escaped Vietnam.*

Source: The author's family archive

*We still have that shirt. Tell me about it.*
I loathed that shirt from the moment I saw it and refuse to believe that somehow it "worked," that it helped you survive. In truth, it probably put us all in more danger.

It was your grandmother's doing. She was very much against our escape. She thought it was too dangerous. But as tough as she was, your grandmother was never one to challenge fate. I, on the other hand, couldn't live under the communists who had designated us *nguy*, which means we were traitors, dishonest, despicable, losers.

But because she loved you and your brother so dearly, your grandmother helped pay for our journey. And with the same love, she bought you those shirts.

This did not, however, occur to me when she brought them to us.

At that time, when we were trying desperately to keep our plans secret, your grandmother headed off to buy those shirts without a travel permit, without informing us, following some hearsay, and probably blathering to every *cyclo* driver and bystander on the way that her son's family was going to *vuot bien*, flee the country.

At a Cho Lon temple, she divulged everything to the head nun, who she hardly knew and who we could not trust. The nun told her that they cared for orphans who were hardy and who had been blessed by the Buddha. Their hardiness and blessings, she said, could be passed on to you and your brother through the saffron-colored shirts that they wore. Knowing that your grandmother would offer a sizable donation, the nun promised that the shirts would provide more protection on our journey than any life jacket.

I can't recall what I said to your grandmother when she presented me with the shirts. Maybe I yelled at her. I was under terrible strain, but I regret that being one of the last exchanges we had together.

And that's another reason why I can't abide that shirt of yours.

*What else do you remember about the journey?*
I haven't mentioned when our boat crashed. It was on the first night, before we even left Vietnamese waters.

We'd been waiting at Rach Gia port for a week, hiding in a filthy little hut. That's where you got really sick. For all that time, your mother held you and sang lullabies and folk songs.

Then finally, we were told to board the boat, but again we waited, this time for another boat to join us, and to be led by the coast guard into international waters. There was no moon. No stars. Just darkness. And I remember admiring how the Socialist Republic of Vietnam was not only letting us go but escorting us to freedom. So it was with relief that I fell asleep on the deck.

Not long afterwards, I woke with a mighty jolt. I've since wondered about how two boats—none more or less seaworthy than the other—could crash in such a way that one would be undamaged, while ours would end up with a hole the size of a large jackfruit in its hull. The hole was not far from where I was sitting. We were fortunate that the hole was just above the water line and that only one person below deck suffered head injuries. But we could not carry on.

The coast guard let the other boat sail into international waters and escorted us back to Son Rai Island where the boat could be repaired. In 2023, Son Rai Island is something of a tourist destination. In 1979, many of the fishing families from the Island had escaped, so it was deserted and there was no shortage of houses in which we could lodge.

That night, when I took you from your mother, I saw that your arms poked out of your tiny yellow shirt. They were as skinny as my fingers. I felt how light you were, and how close you were to leaving us.

I'm not sure whether it was reason or desperation that took hold of me, but the next morning, I asked the owner of the place where we were staying for help.

"This is my baby boy, Kim. He's famished and will not survive. Can you look after him, just until he's stronger? Then, when it's safe, take him back to Saigon, to my mother. I'll give you my wedding ring. And my wife's ring too. Please take him. I'm begging you."

She thought about it, but refused. And there was no time to find someone else because our boat was ready to go again.

What I'm trying to tell you, my son, is that when we escaped Vietnam, I had to make choices. I don't regret them, because I felt like I had no choice. But sometimes, at night, that's what I think about.

*

*Mum, can you respond to what Dad has said?*
Of course, your father has gotten many things wrong.
   I know exactly how he sleeps, what haunts him, and how he is.
   It's true, he's never slept well. And he's up a lot nowadays, because of his racing mind and active bladder. Sometimes he says he lies awake all night. But I'm right next to him. I can hear him breathing. And I can tell you that he sleeps okay.
   Your father exaggerates. He's always been like that.
   I know wives who say their husbands totally change after having a stroke or dementia. Suddenly, a man who was placid is full of rage or a thoughtful and kind husband turns selfish. This is not the case with your father. His stroke has made him more himself: more frantic, more determined.
   No one knows entirely what goes on in your father's head. But I've got a good idea after fifty years of trying to calm him.
   I tell him what's in the past has passed. I remind him that we've had a good life and have nothing to worry about. The news makes him anxious, so I tell him that there's nothing he can do about Putin's invasion of Ukraine. Nor can he sail to the Spratly and Paracel Islands and hold back the Chinese navy. The world is fine. And even if it isn't, it's for young people to sort out now.
   But your father can't rest. His will—to study, to work, to support his family, to fight, to live—continues to astonish me. But it's taken a toll.

*Has it taken a toll on you?*
Well, I'm his wife. If he can't sleep, then I can't either. But I'm used to napping in the day if need be.

Of course, it's not easy now that your father needs care. But it wasn't easy when you were a baby either. Back then, I looked after you. Now, I stay up looking after him.

But let me tell you about your shirt. Because your father's not right about that either.

I've never believed that it had magical powers. It wasn't blessed by Buddha. Who cares if it was? And who knows whether some orphan ever wore it?

But it's not just a worthless rag either.

Your father, he only sees the shirt's cost, its material value.

I'm not sure he's ever noticed the stitching, but if he did, he'd point out that it's uneven. And he might lament that it was sewn by hand, because there were so few sewing machines and overlockers after the war. The communists repossessed them, and when sewing machines broke, there were no spare parts to get them going again. For him, the shirt represents the sanctions, backwardness, and poverty imposed on our homeland.

But the fact that it was handmade is also a sign of our resilience.

So yes. Your shirt *is* precious to me. I know it very well. In 1977, I held you in my womb for nine months. Then in 1979, I held you in my arms for nine months more, when you were wearing that shirt.

As I look at it now, the stitching remains strong, even if it's crooked. The fabric is intact, even its edges are tattered. And in my view, it's still vibrant, despite the stains.

*Is there anything else that Dad said that you want to dispute?*

If we're revisiting history, the truth is your father never consulted me when we were on Son Rai Island about sending you back to Saigon.

He said afterwards that the landlady told him there was no guarantee she could get to Saigon and find your grandmother without a travel permit. It would have been easier, she said, for her to follow us by boat and track us down in some refugee camp.

I suspect she didn't want the weight on her conscience of you dying. Looking back, we should have just given her our wedding rings, because they were the first things the pirates took.

*Did you say anything when you found out that Dad tried to give me away? And why did you bring your wedding rings when you knew there would be pirates?*
I said nothing to your father about it. I wasn't happy, of course. But it didn't matter. We were on our way. And your father was under so much stress. I wasn't about to add to that.

In any case, I can tell you now, if the landlady had accepted his offer, I wouldn't have let you go.

As for the wedding rings, we took them because they were precious to us. They symbolized our love and commitment. It was that simple.

And just as simply, when the pirates pointed their knives at us, we gave them up. In that instant, and in many that followed, we were concerned only with staying alive and keeping you and your brother safe.

So I don't regret anything that I brought or lost.

*What was it like for you on the boat?*
As you sit there now, it's hard to explain how scared I was.

Every choice—Should I feed you this or that? Should I cradle you or set you down? Should I let you crawl on the floor or force you to stay on the mat?—could have made the difference between keeping and losing you. At the same time, I felt powerless with the tangled mass of people around me, as our boat was thrown from one wave to another.

You know that we made it, and today we are safe in our house with a fridge full of food. But back then, I didn't know anything. I was always frightened, so terribly afraid.

I did have a moment of courage. And I'm glad your father still savors that soup.

I certainly recall wobbling more like a clown than an acrobat on the outside ledge of the boat. As I juggled you and the soup, it struck me how foolish I was to take such a risk. I stopped, breathed, and told myself that all I had to do was slide one foot away from the other and then bring them together again.

After I forced my way onto the deck, I called out for your father and, when I found him, stood tall and valiant with the still-warm rice soup in hand. I'll never forget your father and brother looking up at me and saying in unison, "I'm soooo hungry."

After they'd eaten, we took you boys to the edge of the boat and peeled off your dirty shirts and shorts. Then we reached over the edge and bathed you in the streaming water. Someone warned, "Watch out for sharks!" But the ocean was as still and clear as glass, so we were sure we could see any incoming threats. Feeling the sea spray over his body, your brother giggled with delight. You, on the other hand, didn't react all that much.

*Figure 7.3: The Huynh family's spoon.*

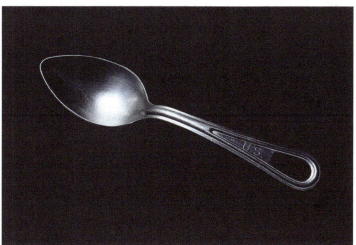

Source: The author's family archive

*What happened to my brother's shirt?*
I don't remember. He was terribly sick too, but not for as long or as bad as you.

We probably lost it in the refugee camp. I got lost myself in that winding maze of tents and tracks.

We also lost two sky-blue outfits that I had sewn for you. Our neighbors said you and your brother looked like adorable Russian dolls when you wore them.

That was the only compliment we received. Even after you two had recovered, you would cry out all day and night. Especially you. "Oh Mum. Oh Dad. Oh Mum. Oh Dad." Our house was not so affectionately known as "Oh Mum and oh Dad's house." Of course, it wasn't a house, but rather a tent made of four sticks and a tarpaulin.

One day, I hung the blue outfits out to dry, and when I turned around, they were gone. Weeks later, I saw them hanging by another tent and took them back. Then someone snatched them again from us and I never saw them again. I imagine the same thing happened to your brother's yellow shirt. Maybe your shirt was so small, ragged, and dirty that nobody wanted it. That's why it's still with us.

*What else is still with us from Vietnam?*
There's the spoon. The one you and your brother as teenagers used to eat cereal in the morning and ice cream at night.

It was never special or treasured, even though it was the last thing that we took from Saigon.

You know, for weeks I thought about what to pack. Carefully, I sewed all the money we had in the world into the seams of my shirt and to the front of your father's trousers. I made an energy powder by soaking sugar with lemon juice and drying it again. All of it was soon gone, but still we have your shirt, and that spoon, which I never wanted anyway.

It was the morning of 19 April 1979 when we said goodbye. We stayed the night at your grandmother's house. Neither your father nor I slept very much.

Your grandmother's heart was breaking, but she was very strong. On the doorstep, she kissed you and your brother and announced loudly that we were off home to see my mother, who was living with us at the time. If the neighbors were watching, they wouldn't have suspected a thing.

Your grandmother remembered that she had boiled some eggs for you boys and asked your aunt to fetch them. I too remembered that I didn't have anything to feed you with and asked for a spoon. Perhaps your aunt was so overwhelmed with emotion that she didn't think and grabbed the first thing that came to hand. In any case, she returned with the stainless-steel US Army spoon that had been used to boil the eggs. It was far too big to feed you with. But I was in no mood for delay, so I threw the spoon into my bag, thinking that I'd replace it with a more suitable one.

Little did I know that we would use that relic from the war in the camp not only to feed you and your brother, but also to cook meals, dig holes, and scale fish.

If you had asked me to choose two things that I could keep from our escape, that shirt and spoon would not be on my list. But they mean a great deal to me now because of the memories they hold.

*You can listen on ABC Radio Canberra to Kim's parents describe* "What it was like on the boat" *and his father recount surviving his stroke in* "I have to live."

*Figure 7.4: UNHCR Displaced Persons Registration Card*

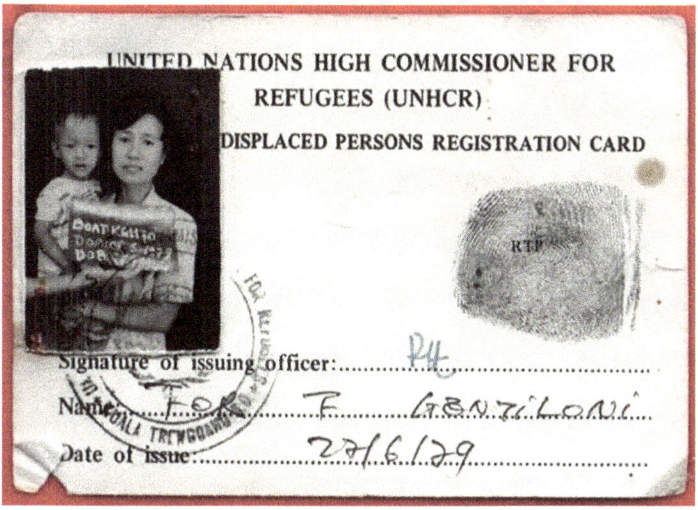
UNITED NATIONS HIGH COMMISSIONER FOR REFUGEES (UNHCR)

DISPLACED PERSONS REGISTRATION CARD

RTP

Signature of issuing officer: ..........

Name: ..........F. GENTILONI..........

Date of issue: ..........27/6/79..........

Source: The author's family archive

# Acknowledgments

The editor gratefully acknowledges the deeply personal contributions made to *What We Brought with Us* by displaced scholars and cultural producers supported by Academy in Exile. Their intimate stories and precious things are a testimony to their resilience and generosity under adversity. The work of the exhibition co-curator Annika Roux and photographer Jobst von Kunowski has been instrumental in the realization of this project. My thanks are due, too, to Kate Bonansinga, Gisela Ecker, Kim Huynh, and Alma-Elisa Kittner for their various contributions to the study of material culture, collecting and archiving, forced migration, border studies, museum and art exhibition, and memory and commemoration.

In its various iterations as traveling exhibition, digital exhibition, and book, the *What We Brought with Us* project has benefited from the care, industry, and expertise of many people. Among those I would like to thank are Kate Bonansinga, Aaron Cohen, Frangis Dadfar Spanta, Çağan Duran, Aaron Fai, Michael Hahn, Kira Heetpass, Vera Hildenbrandt, Sean Keating, Kader Konuk, Jobst von Kunowski, Amy Lind, Jan Lüdert, Erin Maher, Sandra Moreno, Priya Nayar, Egemen Özbek, Matthias Rischau, Annika Roux, Karen Shire, Lydia Schmuck, Jenni Kim Sutmoller, Claudia Tazreiter, Jota Vega, and Davut Yeşilmen. My thanks also go to Sefa Agnew. Support provided by Academy in Exile, Technische Universität Dortmund, Universität Duisburg-Essen, Freie Universität Berlin, Forum Transregionale Studien, Kulturwissenschaftliches Institut Essen, University Alliance Ruhr, University of Cincinnati, Goethe-Institut New York, German Center for Research and Innovation New

York, Deutsches Literaturarchiv Marbach, Literaturhaus Berlin, and Scholars at Risk has allowed the project to reach a wide audience. Generous funding has been provided by the Allianz Foundation, Mellon Foundation, Open Society Foundations, Consortium of Humanities Centers and Institutes, and VolkswagenStiftung. To all, my heartful thanks for helping to bring to light work that advocates on behalf of displaced, threatened, and marginalized people the world over.

# Contributor Biographies

## Academy in Exile Contributors

A.A., Myanmar
M.A., Syria
C.D., Turkey
D.D., Turkey
A.E., Turkey
B.E., Turkey
**Fırat Erdoğmuş**, Turkey
M.G., Turkey
S.H., Israel/O.P.T.
O.H., Turkey
A.J., India
K.K., Iraq
T.K., Poland
A.L., Hong Kong
N.M., Afghanistan
S.M., Afghanistan
D.M., Hungary
A.M., Iran
S.O., Pakistan
E.S., Turkey
Y.U., Turkey
K.Y., Turkey

**Vanessa Agnew** is Professor in the Faculty of Cultural Studies at Technische Universität Dortmund, Associate Director of Academy in Exile, and Honorary Professor in the Humanities Research Centre at The Australian National University. Agnew's *Enlightenment Orpheus: The Power of Music in Other Worlds* (Oxford, 2008) won the Oscar Kenshur Prize and the American Musicological Society's Lewis Lockwood Award. The recipient of research grants from the Alexander von Humboldt Foundation and German Academic Exchange Service, Agnew has co-edited *Settler and Creole Reenactment* (Palgrave, 2010), *Criticism* 46 (2004) and *Rethinking History* 11 (2007), *Refugee Routes* (transcript, 2020), *The Routledge Handbook of Reenactment Studies* (Routledge, 2020), and *Reenactment Case Studies* (Routledge, 2023). Agnew is PI on grants from the Mellon Foundation, Open Society Foundations, and Allianz Foundation to support Academy in Exile. In 2022, Agnew launched *Ostrakon* to publish articles on forced migration and climate issues. Co-curated exhibitions include *Right to Arrive* (Canberra, 2018), *Fixing What's Broken* (Berlin, 2023), and *What We Brought with Us* (Re:Writing the Future Festival, 2021; German Literature Archive Marbach, 2022; Goethe-Institut New York and University of Cincinnati, 2023; *Dengê min tê te? Hörst du mich? Festival für kurdische Exilliteratur*, Literaturhaus Berlin; and Vilnius Old Town Hall, 2024). Agnew's *Wir schaffen das – We'll Make It* (Sefa Verlag, 2021) has been translated into Ukrainian, Arabic, and Farsi. Agnew's current projects are λεῖμμα *(leîmma): Remnantal Responses to Flight* and *Garden(s) of Refuge*.

**Kate Bonansinga** is Director of the School of Art in the College of Design, Architecture, Art, and Planning at the University of Cincinnati, where she is also a professor teaching courses in contemporary art curatorial practice and art in public space. She serves as Faculty Fellow of Cultural Engagement for the university's International Office of Global Initiatives. Bonansinga was the founding director of the Stanlee and Gerald Rubin Center for the Visual Art at the University of Texas at El Paso, where she curated dozens of exhibitions and established an undergraduate minor in museum studies. She is the author of *Curating at the Edge: Artists Respond to the U.S./Mexico Border* (University of Texas

Press, 2014) and of numerous articles, book chapters, and exhibition publication essays, all of which address contemporary art, its meaning, and its purpose. She served as guest curator of *Tania Candiani: Sounding Labor, Silent Bodies* (Contemporary Arts Center, 2020–21) and *American Painting: The Eighties Revisited* (Cincinnati Art Museum, 2021–22) and as author of *The Performing Jewelry of Rachelle Thiewes: Color, Feminism and the Body* (Metal Museum, 2023).

**Gisela Ecker** is Professor (emerita) of Comparative Literature at the Universität Paderborn. She has also taught at Ludwig Maximilian Universität in Munich, the Universität zu Köln, Goethe Universität in Frankfurt, and the University of Sussex; and held visiting professorships at the University of Cincinnati; Emory University; the University of California, Berkeley; and Columbia University. She has published in the fields of German and English literature on cultural and gender studies, travel literature, and material cultural studies. Among her monographs and coedited volumes are *Schemata und Praktiken* (Fink, 2012); *Kulturen der Arbeit* (Fink, 2011); *'Giftige' Gaben. Über Tauschprozesse in der Literatur* (Fink, 2008); *In Spuren reisen. Vor-Bilder und Vor-Schriften in der Reiseliteratur* (LIT-Verlag, 2006); *Dinge. Medien der Aneignung – Grenzen der Verfügung* (Helmer, 2002); *Sammeln – Ausstellen – Wegwerfen* (Helmer, 2001); *UmOrdnungen der Dinge* (Helmer, 2000); *Kein Land in Sicht. Heimat – weiblich?* (Fink, 1997); "Everyday Life," special issue, *Journal for the Study of British Cultures* 6 no. 2 (1999); and *Feminist Aesthetics* (Beacon Press, 1986).

**Kim Huynh** is a teacher, writer, researcher, and broadcaster who helps everyday people tell their extraordinary stories. His latest book, *Australia's Refugee Politics in the 21st Century* (Routledge, 2023), reviews this topic and develops ways to enhance national security, refugee rights, and social cohesion. Huynh has published a collection of stories about contemporary Vietnam entitled *Vietnam as if...* (ANU Press, 2015). His biography of his parents, *Where the Sea Takes Us* (HarperCollins, 2007), attracted academic and literary attention. He co-authored *Children and Global Conflict* (Cambridge, 2015) and co-edited *The Culture Wars: Australian and American Politics in the 21st Century* (Palgrave Macmillan, 2009).

He facilitates discussions on culture and ideas with the Vietnamese Australia Forum, coordinates a current affairs discussion group for rough sleepers, and writes essays on a wide range of topics for news outlets. Huynh ran as an independent candidate in the 2016 Australian Capital Territory election and in the 2022 Australian federal election. He is a presenter at ABC Radio Canberra and Deputy Director of the Australian National University's Humanities Research Centre.

**Alma-Elisa Kittner** is an art historian and senior lecturer in the Institute of Art Education at the Justus-Liebig-Universität Gießen. From 2020 to 2022, she was the spokesperson for the Research Group "Art Production and Art Theory in the Age of Global Migration" (with Kerstin Meincke and Miriam Oesterreich), and she was a member of the Deutsche Forschungsgemeinschaft network "Entangled Histories of Art and Migration: Forms, Visibilities, Agents." She received her doctorate in 2005, published as *Visuelle Autobiographien. Sammeln als Selbstentwurf bei Hannah Höch, Sophie Calle und Annette Messager* (2009). She held doctoral and postdoctoral fellowships in the research groups "The Staging of the Body" and "Interart Studies" at the Freie Universität Berlin. Her current research project analyzes modern and contemporary artists' travels to Italy with a focus on Italy's position within Mediterranean migration. Her publications include *La Méditerranée – zeitgenössische Perspektiven auf den Mittelmeerraum* (with Gabriele Genge), *kritische berichte* 4 (2017); and "Objects of Migration: On Archives and Collections, Archivists and Collectors," *Visual Anthropology* 34, no. 4 (2021). For the upcoming publication *Entangled Histories of Art and Migration* (ed. Cathrine Bublatzky, Burcu Dogramaci, and Mona Schieren), she curated the section Materiality | Materialisation with Buket Altinoba, including her essay "On Materiality, Migration, and the Arts." Her latest research interests focus on Jewish perspectives in the visual arts.

**Jobst von Kunowski** is a visual artist and photographer. He studied fine arts in the department of photography and painting at the Academy of Fine Arts Leipzig, Germany. In his work, von Kunowski deals with urban living spaces and people's individual characteristics, developing a visual language that combines documentary and fictional elements. His work has been shown in a range of venues, including the group exhibition and publication *Psychoscape: Periphery and Photography* (2002) and the exhibition *anlanden* in the Laden für Nichts Gallery in Leipzig (2005). Since 2015, he has been photographing public spaces in Berlin's Neukölln neighborhood. For the publication *Wilhelm von Humboldt in Tegel. Ein Bildprogramm als Bildungsprogramm* (2018), von Kunowski produced interior views of the Humboldt Castle in Berlin Tegel. Since 2017, von Kunowski has been working with the team of Academy in Exile. Some of the resulting work, a series of portrait photographs of the Fellows, cannot be shown due to political sensitivities. For the exhibition and publication *What We Brought with Us*, von Kunowski photographed people's treasured possessions to show the objects in their true light. A selection of von Kunowski's work is published at jobstvonkunowski.de.

**Amy Lind** is Mary Ellen Heintz Professor of Women's, Gender, and Sexuality Studies at the University of Cincinnati (UC). Since 2019, she has also served as Director of UC's Taft Research Center. In this capacity, she also serves on the international executive board of the Consortium of Humanities Centers and Institutes (2020–present). As an interdisciplinary scholar trained in urban studies and design, critical development studies, Latin American studies, postcolonial/decolonial studies, and feminist and queer studies, she has focused her research on how people navigate and resist political-economic hegemonies. Her first book, *Gendered Paradoxes: Women's Movements and the Politics of Global Development in Ecuador* (Penn State University Press, 2005), focuses on the contradictions of women's politicized encounters with modernity and the post–World War II global development industry. Since then, she has edited four volumes and published numerous journal articles and book chapters. Her forthcoming book, co-authored with political theorist Christine Keating, focuses on Ecuador's political project to reconstitute the postcolonial nation as plurinational and postcapitalist. She is co-Editor-in-Chief of the *International Feminist Journal of Politics*. She is also working on a larger research project documenting the role of transnational solidarity in resistance to the Chilean dictatorship

(1973–1990), including through the political activism and photography of her "aunt" Amy Conger.

**Annika Roux** is completing a bachelor's degree in media and communication studies at Freie Universität Berlin, while also pursuing a master's degree in Romance literature with a focus on Spanish and Portuguese philology. She was responsible for the creative realization of the exhibition *Lorca – Views on a Global Reception* at the Spanish Embassy (2019) and Instituto Cervantes Frankfurt (2019), and the technical realization of a series of talks entitled *Students Read Contemporary Spanish-Language Literature*, directed by Susanne Zepp. She studied furniture and object design at the Universidad de las Américas in Santiago, Chile. From 2019 until 2023, she was a member of the production team at Academy in Exile, where she managed the website and contributed to conference organizing, the e-learning video series, and the layout of publications such as Academy in Exile's short-form imprint, *Ostrakon*. Additionally, Roux was the co-curator of the exhibition *What We Brought with Us*, first shown digitally as part of the *Re:Writing the Future Festival* (2021) and subsequently at the German Literature Archive Marbach (2022), the University of Cincinnati, the Goethe-Institut New York (2023), and elsewhere. In February 2023, she started working at Freie Universität Berlin as a student advisor in the Institute of Romance Philology.

# Index

**A**
Academia de Guerra de la Fuerza Áerea de Chile (FACH) detention center, 149-150
academic freedom, 20
Academy in Exile, **53–131**
Adidjatou, Bella, 147
Adler, H. G., 16-17
Afghanistan, 64, 100, 108
African American history, 23
agency, 18, 23
Agnew, Vanessa, **13–26**, 53
Allende, Salvador, 151, 152, 153
Amnesty International, 152
amulet, 124-125
Anderson, Jack, 150-151
antiquities, 19, 27-28
anxiety, 86, 168
apodemic, 18
Appadurai, Arjun, 21, 43-44, 134, 142
Archaeological Museum Frankfurt, 32-33

archaeology, 19, 32-33
archives, 21, 23, 32-33
Armenia, 70
*arpilleras*, 155
arrival, 15, 19, 116, 122
art market, 133, 142
artistic production, 20, 133-134, 137-139, 141, 143, 145, 146-148
ashes. *See* human remains (ashes)
asylum, 19, 22
at-risk scholars, 20, 53
aura, 31, 46
Australia, 159
Austria, 27, 29-30, 29
authoritarianism, 20, 54, 60, 149-153
"Autobiographical Stories" (Calle), 35-38, 35
autobiography, 35-38

**B**
Baeck, Leo, 13 n.1
bags, 16, 23, 48, 110-111
beaches, 22-23, 159

Benjamin, Walter, 22 n.7
Bhutan, 141, *144*
biographies of things, 18, 45- 46
biometric data gathering, 22
blacklisting, 152
boat journey, 159, 163- 168, 170- 171
boatpeople, 159, 163- 165, 166- 173
Bonansinga, Kate, 20, **133–148**
book burning, 29
books, 27, 29, 34, 47, 94- 97, 155
border crossing, 19, 44, 46, 48, 137
borders, 19, 137- 139, 146
Bourriaud, Nicholas, 145
Boym, Svetlana, 48
Brown, Bill, 134, 139, 142, 145. See also Thing Theory (Brown)
Buckley, William F., 151
Buddhism, 142, 166, 169
*By the Sea* (Gurnah), 18- 19, 20

**C**
Calle, Sophie, 21, 35- 38, *35*
Casa de Paz, 137
cataloguing, 17- 18, 23. See also inventories
ceremonial objects, 31, 33
Charents, Yeghishe, 70
childhood, 15 n.2, 16, 36, 46, 56, 58, 88, 108, 118, 164- 165, 167, 170- 173
Chile, 19, 21, 149- 156
Cincinnati, 41, 54, 137, 140, 141, *144*. See also Wave Pool
clothing, 47, 48, 56- 65, 68- 69, 165- 167, 169. See also jewelry; shoes

Cold War, 150- 151
collaboration, 20, 137- 138, 141, 143- 145, 146- 148
collectibility, 134
collection, 19, 21, 27- 31, 36- 37, 38, 49
colonial collection, 19, 21, 27- 28 n.1
commemoration, 155- 156
commodification, 45, 133, 134, 142, 148
communication, 20, 33, 43
communism, 151, 162, 166, 169
community building, 133, 138, 141, 145, 147- 148
concentration camps, 13, 15- 17
  Auschwitz, 15
  Freiberg, 15
  Mauthausen, 15
  Stutthof, 17
  Terezín (Theresienstadt), 13, 15, 16
confiscation, 15, 16- 17, 163
Conger, Amy, 19, 21, 149- 156, *154*
conjecture, 22
Contemporary Arts Center (Cincinnati), 141
contingency planning, 15, 22
couch, Freud's, 28, 29- 31, *35*, 36- 37
craft, 133, 137- 138, 142, 143, 145
crimes against humanity, 151
Cruz, Marelin, *135–136*
Cullen, Calgano (Cal), 133, 143, 145, 147
Cullen, Geoffrey (Skip), 133

cultural heritage, 23
Czech Republic, 13- 16
Czechowicz, Józef, 104

**D**
Daston, Lorraine, 43, 49
*débrouillard*, 22
decolonization, 27- 28 n.1. *See also* colonial collection
dementia, 159, 161- 162, 168- 169
democracy, 20, 60- 61, 151
departure, 22, 53, 78, 80, 102, 163, 172- 173
deportation, 13- 17, 33, 139, 153
detention, 149- 153
deterritorialization, 43
diaspora, 31, 31- 32, 32, 48, 49, 139
Dicker-Brandeis, Friedl, 15 n.2
dictatorship, 149- 153. *See also* authoritarianism; post-dictatorship
disappearance, 21, 150, 152, 156
displacement, 18, 19- 20, 22- 23, 44, 48, 137, 139, 146, 155
disposable objects, 47, 114- 115
dispossession, 16- 17
divan. *See* couch, Freud's
dogs, 112- 113, 154- 155
"double exile," 19, 150- 152

**E**
Ecker, Gisela, 20- 21, **41–51**
El Salvador, 137
embroidery, 23, 34, 100- 101, 135–136, 137- 138, 140, 141

emigration, 27- 30, 152- 153. *See also* immigration; migration
emplacement, 18, 22, 53
Erdoğmuş, Fırat, 68
ethnographic artifacts, 19, 21, 27- 28
everyday life, 33- 34, 45- 47, 49- 50, 145
evidence, 23, 32- 33
exchange, 134
execution, 149, 152, 155, 156
exhibitions, 27- 28 n.1, 31- 34, 36- 37, 41- 42, 53- 54, 141- 142. *See also* museums; *What We Brought with Us*
exile, 18- 21, 27- 30, 37, 43- 45, 46- 50, **53–131**, 152- 153, 154- 155
Expo Chicago, 133, 138, *138*
extermination camps, 17. *See also* concentration camps

**F**
family, 13- 16, 21, 34, 92- 93, 155- 156, 160, 162- 173
Federal Office for Migration and Refugees (BAMF), 22
Feierstein, Liliana Ruth, 31
fieldwork, 48, 49
Fittko, Lisa, 22 n.7
flags, 104- 105, 108- 109
flight, 18, 22- 23, 27- 28, 33- 34, 38, 44, 74, 163- 166, 172- 173. *See also* departure; exile
food, 15, 164- 165, 170- 171, 172- 173

forced migration, 18, 20, 27- 30, 33- 34, 53, 74, 80, 133. *See also* exile; flight; refugees
forgetting, 32- 33, 34, 44, 90
France, 36, 162
Freud, Sigmund, 19, 21, 27- 32, 29, 35- 38
Freud Museum (London), 28- 30, 36
friendship, 64, 68, 76, 84- 92, 96- 98, 114, 124- 126, 130, 155
future, 14- 15, 20, 22, 44, 48- 49

**G**

Galindo, Guillermo, 146
Gaza, 23
genocide
    Armenia, 70
    Gaza, 23
    Holocaust/Shoah, 13- 17, 32- 34, 37- 38
German, Vanessa, 143- 146, 144
Germany, 20, 32- 34, 38, 53, 82, 94- 96, 98, 102, 104. *See also What We Brought with Us*
Gibson, Jeffrey, 146, 147
gifts, 47, 64, 68, 72- 78, 84- 86, 90, 96, 120- 126, 130
Girth, Jake, 137
Goethe-Institut New York, 41, 54
grief. *See* mourning
Gurnah, Abdulrazak, 18- 19, 20
Gurung, Sita, *140*, 147

**H**

Habermas, Tilmann, 47
Hague Convention for the Protection of Cultural Property in the Event of Armed Conflict (1954), 23
Harman, Graham, 134, 139. *See also* Object Oriented Ontology (Harman)
Haug, Helgard, 32- 33
*Heimat*, 44
"hermeneutics of baggage" (Gurnah), 19
Holocaust, 13- 17, 32- 34, 37- 38
home, 48, 70, 100- 102, 108
homelessness, 118
Hong Kong, 60
hope, 47, 53, 64, 70, 74, 126, 153, 163
Hošková-Weissová, Helga. *See* Weissová, Helga
hospitality, 104
host countries, 16- 17, 20
household items, 34, 49
human remains (ashes), 21, 149, 156
hunger, 164- 165, 170- 171. *See also* food
Huynh, Kim, 19- 20, **159–173**, *160*, *165*, *173*

**I**

illness, 15, 164- 165, 167, 168- 169, 170- 171
immigration, 19, 110, 137. *See also* emigration; migration

imprisonment, 15, 149-153
incarceration. *See* imprisonment
Independent Art Fair (New York City), 133, 145
India, 94, 128, 130, 139
inheritance, 82, 128
inner emigration, 152-153
installations, 18 n.4, 35-38, 134
intangible heritage, 23
inventories, 13-15, 16-19, 20-23
Israel, 23
itinerancy, 18

**J**
jewelry, 74-75, 80-83, 122-123, 167, 169-170
Jewish Museum Berlin, 33-34
Jewish Museum Frankfurt, 32-33
Jewish objects, 30-34, 38
Jewish studies, 30-34
Jewishness, 21, 30-34, 37-38, 104-105
journeys, 74, 116, 120, 126, 159, 163-168, 170-171

**K**
Kaléko, Mascha, 13, 23
*kalmeez*, 64-65
Kashmir, 88, 141
*see* Khan, Baseera, 139–143, 140
Kilpper, Thomas, 18 n.4
Kissinger, Henry, 151
Kittner, Alma-Elisa, 19, 21, 23, **27–40**
knowledge production, 18

Koch, Gertrud, 30
Kopytoff, Igor, 45
Kugelmann, Cilly, 30, 31
Kunowski, Jobst von, 20, **53–131**

**L**
Latour, Bruno, 49
LGBTQIA, 104-105, 118, 141
Limbu, Bishnu, *140*, *147*
Limbu, Durga, *140*
Lind, Amy, 19, 20, 21, **149–157**
"List of Possessions" (Weissová), 13-15, *14*, 16
lists. *See* inventories
Literaturhaus Berlin, 54
litotes, 23
Liu, Peiyu, 137
locality, 21, 43-45
London, 27-30, 49
longing, 48, 148. *See also* nostalgia
loss, 16-17, 32, 46, 48, 50. *See also* mourning
love, 62, 74, 166, 170
luggage, 16-17, 19, 42, 66, 94

**M**
makers, 20, 133, 137-138, 141, 143, 145-148
Malaysia, 164
Martinez, Elia, *135–136*
material culture, 18, 20-21, 42-43
mementoes, 43-45, 48, 56, 78
memory, 28, 33-38, 90, 112, 155-156
Mexico, 138-139, 146, 152

migrants, 133, 137, 146- 148. *See also* migration
migration, 18- 23, 29- 30, 32- 34, 44. *See also* emigration; exile; forced migration; immigration; migrants
Miles, Tiya, 23
military coups
 Chile, 21, 148- 153, 155- 156
 Myanmar, 106
Miller, Daniel, 49
misbaha, 128- 131
Molina, Lorena, 135–136, 137- 139
mourning, 47, 162. *See also* loss
Movimiento de Izquierda Revolucionaria (MIR), 152, 154- 155, 156
Muhammed Ali, Taha, 23
musealization, 21, 27- 29, 38
museums, 28- 30, 32- 34, 36- 37, 142- 143
music, 15, 23, 167
Muslim Americans, 139- 141
Myanmar, 106

**N**
narration, 23, 36- 37
National Literaturarchiv Marbach, 41, 54
Native American art, 146
*nazar boncuğu*, 124- 125
Nazis, 17, 27- 28, 32- 33
neighborhood, 44- 45, 50
New Institutionalism, 146 n.6
Nigeria, 144

nostalgia, 48, 90

**O**
object biography, 18, 45- 46
"Object Days" (Jewish Museum Berlin), 33- 34
Object Oriented Ontology (Harman), 134, 139, 145. *See also* Harman, Graham
objects, 17- 18, 27- 34, 37- 38, 41- 45, 46- 50, 134, 139. *See also* inventories; Object Oriented Ontology (Harman); things
objects in/of exile, 18 n.5
objects of migration, 32- 34
objects of transition, 43- 45. *See also* transitional objects (Winnicott)
Olludare, Michael, 143
oral history, 151- 152, **159–173**

**P**
packing, 22, 62, 68, 94, 102, 122, 172- 173
paintings, 13- 16, 102- 103
Pakistan, 110
Palestine, 23, 76
papers (official), 22- 23, 94, 163
Parkin, David, 21, 44, 47
parting, 84, 128
passports, 16
past, 14- 15, 21, 32- 33, 37, 44, 47- 49, 162, 168. *See also* memory
performance art, 134

Philip M. Meyers Jr. Memorial Gallery, University of Cincinnati, 41
phones, 47-48, 106-107
photography, 27-28, 42, **53–131**, 137-138, 153, 156
Poland, 104
ports, 166-167
possessions, 13-19, 20-23, 27-29, 53, 155, 159. See also inventories; objects; things
post-dictatorship, 150, 153-156. See also dictatorship
Prague, 13-16
prayer, 128-132, 137, 140, 141, 142
precarity, 20
preparation for leaving, 13-17, 22, 27-28, 163-164, 166, 172-173. See also inventories; packing
presents. See gifts
production of locality (Appadurai), 43-45
property declaration form (Nazi), 16-17
protest, 94, 141
provenance, 17
psychoanalysis, 29-30, 35-37
Putnam, James, 27, 28-29, 36

**R**
Rai, Gita, *140*
Rai, Laxmi, *140*
Rai, Phampa, *147*
recontextualization, 43
reenactment, 27-29
refugee camps, 141, 169, 171-172, 173
refugee routes, 19
refugees, 19-20, 133, 141, 146, 159, 163-168, 169-173
*Reichsfluchtsteuer* ("Reich escape tax"), 28
repair, 156
repetition, 27-28, 49
repression, 20, 34-35, 47-48, 106, 152
resilience, 152, 169
resistance, 22 n.7, 134, 146, 152-153
reterritorialization, 43
revolution, 152-155, 161, 162
*Re:Writing the Future Festival*, 41, 54
Ricciado, Massimo, 18 n.4
Rimini Protokoll, 32-33
*rite-de-passage* souvenirs, 47
Rodriguez, Fabiola, *135–136, 140*
Rojas, Jetzabel, *135–136*
roots, 47, 48
Roux, Annika, 20, **53–131**

**S**
"safe country," 116
Said, Edward W., 94-95
Schnure, Rowe, *140, 147*
scholar rescue, 20, 53
sculpture, 142, 143-145, *144*
securitization, 19, 22
Seda-Reder, Maria, 145
selections, 17
Shoah, 13-17, 32-34, 37-38
shoes, 42, 43, 47, 56-57

Shtivelman, Viktoria, 34
Sigmund Freud Museum (Vienna), 30
slavery, 23
smell, 62
social justice, 134, 143, 148
social media, 106, 153, 155- 156
socially engaged art, 145- 146, 147- 148
Sonnemann, Thorsten, 32
Sotelo, Raquel, *135–136*
souvenirs, 42, 45, 47, 48, 58- 59, 70- 71
Soviet Union, 33- 34
space, 20, 28, 31, 42
state violence, 152- 155
stories, 19- 21, 23, 27, 33- 38, 48, 149 n.1, 150- 151, 156
Subba, Kumari, *147*
Subba, Susmita, *147*
superstition, 162
symbolic meaning, 42- 43, 53, 70, 76, 100, 159
Syria, 94, 126, 130

**T**

telling objects (Daston), 20- 21, 42- 43
Terezín (Theresienstadt), 13, 15, 16
territorialization, 43
theft, 15, 53
thick description, 23
Thing Theory (Brown), 134, 139, 145. *See also* Brown, Bill

things, 15- 21, 22- 23, 41, 43, 44, 45- 50, 53, 134, 139. *See also* inventories; objects; Thing Theory (Brown)
time, 14- 15, 18, 20, 42, 44, 72. *See also* future; past
Torah, 33
torture, 21, 149- 150, 152, 155
toys, 16, 47, 48, 86- 87, 118- 119, 139
transitional objects (Winnicott), 46- 48, 50. *See also* objects of transition
transports, 15- 17
trauma, 41, 43, 70, 142, 155
Turkey, 68, 70, 78, 96, 102

**U**

Ugrešić, Dubravka, 46
Ukraine, 34, 104, 168
"Unboxing Past," 32- 33
undocumented, 22- 23
Undocumented Migrant Project, 22- 23
United Kingdom, 27- 30, 49
United Nations High Commissioner for Refugees (UNHCR), *173*
United States, 102, 137- 142, 146, 150- 152
Universidad de Chile, 150, 153

**V**

value, 44- 48, 142, 159, 169
Vienna, 27, 29- 30, 29
Viet Minh, 161, 162

Vietnam, 159, 161-163, 166-168, 172-173
Visionaries and Voices, 143, 144
visual irony, 14-15
*vuot bien* ("cross over," flee the country), 166

**W**
waiting, 138, 167
war, 15, 20, 37-38, 100, 114, 137, 162, 173
War Academy of the Chilean Air Force detention center, 149-150
Wave Pool, 133, 141, 143, 145-146, 147-148. *See also* Welcome Editions
wayfinding, 42
weaving, 140, 141-142, 145, 146, 147
wedding cloth, 34
"Wedding Dress, The" (Calle), 35, 36-38
Weiss, Helga. *See* Weissová, Helga
Weissová, Helga, 13-16, 14
Welcome Editions, 133, 135–136, 137-141, 138, 140, 143, 144, 145-148, 147
*What We Brought with Us*, 20-21, 41-43, 44-45, 46-48, 50, **53–131**
Winnicott, Donald, 46
witnessing, 34, 36, 46, 90, 152-153
women's history, 23
writing, 13-14, 84, 104, 155

**Y**
*yergir* (homeland), 70

**Z**
Zimbabwe, 144
Żmichowska, Narcyza, 104

www.ingramcontent.com/pod-product-compliance
Lightning Source LLC
Jackson TN
JSHW011420110225
78875JS00006B/69